EXCEL 2022

FROM BEGINNER TO EXCEL HACKER.
THE 5-MINUTE A DAY CRASH COURSE WITH PRACTICAL ILLUSTRATED EXAMPLES TO UNLOCK EXCEL POWER, MASTER FORMULAS AND FUNCTIONS, AND CREATE NEW JOB OPPORTUNITIES

BY ALBERT NEWMAN

Table of Contents

TABLE OF CONTENTS 2

INTRODUCTION 9

CHAPTER 1.   EXCEL TERMINOLOGIES 12

    AUTOFORMAT 12

    DATA VALIDATION 12

    PIVOT TABLE 12

    PIVOT MAP 12

    VALUES AREA 12

    ITEM 12

    WORKSHEET 12

    COLUMNS AND ROWS 13

    HEADINGS FOR COLUMNS AND ROWS 13

    WORKSPACE 13

    RANGE OF CELLS 13

    FREEZE PANES 13

    AUTOFILL 14

    AUTOSUM 14

    MERGED CELL 14

    ERROR CODE 14

    WORKBOOK 15

CHAPTER 2.   BASICS OF EXCEL 16

    GETTING STARTED WITH EXCEL 16

    SOME TERMINOLOGIES OF EXCEL 17

    YOU CAN ALSO FORMAT THE CELLS 17

    YOU CAN PERFORM CALCULATIONS 18

    ADDING A CELL AND A ROW 19

    HOW TO USE FORMULAS IN EXCEL 19

    YOU CAN ALSO MAKE A GRAPH IN EXCEL 20

    DATA REPRESENTATION VIA A PIVOT TABLE 20

YOU CAN ADD TEXT, PHOTOS, GRAPHS AND CHARTS TO IMPROVE YOUR SPREADSHEET 21

CONVERT GOOGLE SHEETS INTO AN EXCEL SHEET 22

USE FILTERS TO MAKE WORK EASIER 23

COPY/PASTE A FORMULA 23

ELIMINATE REDUNDANT DATASETS 24

CONVERTING THE ROWS AND COLUMNS 24

YOU CAN ALSO DIVIDE THE DATA FROM ONE CELL TO THE OTHER 24

USE FORMULAS TO SAVE TIME 25

CHANGE THE COLOR OF THE CELLS BY USING CONDITIONAL FORMATTING 25

USE OF IF LOGIC IN EXCEL 26

CHAPTER 3. EXCEL WORKSHEET OPERATIONS 27

INSERTING COLUMNS AND ROWS 27

DELETING COLUMNS AND ROWS 28

CLEAR A CELL'S CONTENTS 28

CUT OR COPY DATA 29

MOVE CELLS BY DRAGGING AND DROPPING 30

HOW TO SELECT CELLS OR RANGES 31

PREVIEW AN ITEM BEFORE PASTING 31

PASTE SPECIAL 32

SETTINGS FOR FORMULAS 32

DELETING DATA AND THE UNDO COMMAND 33

ADJUSTING COLUMNS AND ROWS 34

FIND AND REPLACE 36

CHAPTER 4. GETTING TO KNOW FORMULAS 42

ARITHMETIC FORMULAS 42

FINANCIAL FORMULAS 42

LOOK-UP FORMULAS 42

DEFINING FUNCTIONS IN EXCEL 43

USER-DEFINED FUNCTIONS 43

BUILT-IN FUNCTIONS 43

UNDERSTANDING ARGUMENTS 44

REASONS FOR USING FORMULAS IN EXCEL 45
IMPORTANT THINGS TO KNOW ABOUT FUNCTIONS 45

CHAPTER 5.   EXCEL FORMULAS AND FUNCTIONS 47

ADDITION IN EXCEL SPREADSHEET 47
SUBTRACTION IN EXCEL 49
FINDING AVERAGE 50
MULTIPLICATION IN EXCEL 51
UNDERSTANDING DIVISION IN SPREADSHEET 52
FINDING MINIMUM VALUE 53
HOW TO FIND A MAXIMUM VALUE 54
USING COUNT FORMULA IN EXCEL 55
UNDERSTANDING COUNTA FUNCTION 56
CONCATENATE FUNCTION IN EXCEL 57
FINDING CURRENT DATE AND TIME IN EXCEL 59

CHAPTER 6.   EXCEL FUNCTIONS 60

EXCEL FUNCTIONS – DATE AND TIME 60
EXCEL FUNCTIONS – LOGICAL 61
EXCEL FUNCTIONS – LOOKUP AND REFERENCE 62
EXCEL FUNCTIONS – TEXT FUNCTIONS 64
EXCEL FUNCTIONS – MATH 66

CHAPTER 7.   EXCEL CHARTS 68

THE PIE CHARTS 68
COLUMN GRAPHS 69
THE LINE CHARTS 70
THE AREA CHARTS 71
SCATTER CHARTS 71
BUBBLE CHARTS 73
SURFACE CHARTS 73
RADAR CHARTS 74
COMBO CHARTS 74
EXCEL CHART CUSTOMIZATION 75

How Significant Are the Charts? 75

CHAPTER 8. EXCEL PIVOT TABLE 77

Field List 77

Pivot Table Area 78

The Filter Area 78

The Rows Area 79

The Columns Area 80

The Values Area 80

Using the Commands to Accomplish a Pivot Table 81

Sum Value 84

Count Value 86

Average Value 87

Max Value 87

Min Value 87

Product Value 88

Count Numbers Value 88

StdDev Value 88

Var Value 89

Varp Value 89

Excel Tips for Pivot Tables 90

CHAPTER 9. GETTING MORE IN EXCEL 91

How to Insert Rows and Columns 91

Working on Ribbons 94

Adding Comments in Cells 97

How to View All Comments in a Spreadsheet 98

File Sharing in Excel 99

Adding Notes in Cells 101

Spreadsheet and Workbook Protection 102

Understanding Smart Lookup Feature 104

CHAPTER 10. EXCEL TIPS AND TRICKS 105

1. Search For Templates Online 105

2.	Name Your Worksheets Correctly	105
3.	Define Your Header/Title	105
4.	Dos and Don'ts Of Fonts	106
5.	Create Space For Breathing Room	107
6.	Add An Image	107
7.	Go Off the Grid	107
8.	Zebra Striped	108
9.	Use Tables, Graphs, And Charts	108
10.	Create Cell Styles	109
11.	Show Restraint	109

BONUS: MAKE USE OF AND EARN WITH YOUR EXCEL SKILLS IN WORKSPACE AND MARKETPLACE 110

CONCLUSION 113

©Copyright 2022 - All rights reserved

The content contained within this book may not be reproduced, duplicated, or transmitted without direct written permission from the author or the publisher.

Under no circumstances will any blame or legal responsibility be held against the publisher, or author, for any damages, reparation, or monetary loss due to the information contained within this book, either directly or indirectly.

Legal Notice

This book is copyright protected. This book is only for personal use. You cannot amend, distribute, sell, use, quote or paraphrase any part, or the content within this book, without the consent of the author-publisher.

Disclaimer Notice

Please note the information contained within this document is for educational and entertainment purposes only. All effort has been executed to present accurate, up to date, and reliable, complete information. No warranties of any kind are declared or implied. Readers acknowledge that the author is not engaging in the rendering of legal, financial, medical, or professional advice.

Introduction

Microsoft Excel is a spreadsheet tool created by Microsoft that allows users to organize, organise, and calculate data via the use of mathematical formulas. This software is a component of the Microsoft Office suite, although it can also communicate with other Office applications. Microsoft Excel, like many other Microsoft Office products, is now offered as a cloud-based subscription service via Office 365. Developed by Microsoft, MS Excel is a professional spreadsheet tool that has been produced for use with the Microsoft Windows and Mac OS operating systems, respectively. It provides, among other things, the ability to do basic arithmetic, make use of graphing tools, create pivot tables, and program macros.

Spreadsheet tools such as Microsoft Excel make use of a collection of cells that are grouped into rows and columns in order to actually organize and manage data. They may also display data visually via the use of charts, histograms, and line graphs. Using Microsoft Excel, users may arrange data in order to see different elements from a variety of perspectives. Microsoft Visual Basic is actually a programming language that may be used to create a variety of advanced numerical methods in Microsoft Excel, and it is available for free download. Developers have the option of creating code directly in the Visual Basic Editor, which includes Windows for troubleshooting and organizing code modules.

History and Future of MS Excel

For data analysis and documentation, Microsoft Excel is a useful and capable tool. It's a spreadsheet software with several columns and rows, with each intersection of a column or a row being referred to as a "cell." Each cell carries a single piece of data or information. You may make information simpler to locate and automatically pull information from moving information by arranging the data in this manner. Microsoft Excel played a critical role in accounting and record-keeping for company operations in the initial periods of accessible PC business computing. A table with an autosum format is one of the finest examples of an MS Excel use case. Entering a column of data and clicking into a cell at the end of the spreadsheet, as well as using the "autosum" option to enable that column to add up all of the values input above, is extremely simple with Microsoft Excel. This replaces manual ledger counts, which were a time-consuming aspect of business prior to the development of the contemporary spreadsheet.

Because of the autosum feature and other enhancements, Microsoft Excel has become a must-have for many forms of corporate computing, such as analyzing daily, weekly, or monthly numbers, tabulating payroll or taxes, and doing other equivalent business activities, among other things. Because of a wide range of straightforward application scenarios, Microsoft Excel has emerged as a prominent end-user technology that is useful in training and professional development. Because Microsoft Excel has been included in basic business diploma courses on computer-assisted drafting for a number of years, temporary employment firms may assess people's skills with Microsoft Word and Microsoft Excel in order to hire them for a wide range of clerical jobs.

Microsoft Excel, on the other hand, has become entirely outdated in certain respects as business technology has progressed. This is due to a notion is known as "visual dashboard" technology, sometimes known as "data visualization." In general, businesses and suppliers have devised innovative new methods to graphically display data that do not need end-users to examine a conventional spreadsheet with columns of numbers and IDs. Instead, they use graphs, charts, and other complex displays to better grasp and comprehend the data. People have learned that "reading" a visual presentation is much simpler.

The application cases for Microsoft Excel have changed as a result of the data visualization concept. Whereas in the past, companies may have used Microsoft Excel to manage hundreds of entries, today's commercial use cases often include spreadsheets that handle just a few dozen variables for each project. If the spreadsheet has more than a few dozen rows, the information will be more effective shown on a visual dashboard than in a conventional spreadsheet style.

Spreadsheets, second only to word processors, have become one of the most common types of computer software. Data, mathematical formulae, text, and images may all be combined in a single report and workbook using spreadsheet software. As a result, spreadsheets have become essential commercial tools, as well as being widely used in scientific research. Excel, in particular, has received widespread praise for its simplicity of use and capability. As spreadsheets' power and simplicity of use have grown, there has been a surge in interest in utilizing them in the classroom. Due to the widespread availability of spreadsheet software at colleges and institutions, a statistics teacher may teach a course without asking students to buy extra software. It would be dishonest not to add a few cautions now that we've highlighted Excel's benefits for teaching fundamental statistics. Spreadsheets are not statistics programs. Therefore, their ability to replace a full-featured statistics program is limited. Equitable two-way analysis of variance is simple in Excel, while unequal two-way analysis of variance is difficult. Spreadsheets also have limitations when it comes to processing data with null values.

Who is this book for?

This book is intended for home and corporate users of Microsoft Office applications who wish to utilize Excel to organize their data, produce meaningful studies and visualizations, as well as uncover information into their processes utilizing Excel's extensive business intelligence analytical capabilities. The book's material is intended for individuals who already have already utilized older versions of Excel as well as those who are learning Excel for the very first time.

Chapter 1. Excel Terminologies

AutoFormat

It is software that applies a preset format to cells that meet specific requirements. It may be as essential as font size and alignment.

Data Validation

This function lets you avoid entering inaccurate data into your worksheet. Drop-down lists of common words are most frequently created using this method. Data validation ensures that the data being entered is consistent and accurate.

Pivot Table

It's a data summarization method most widely used to sort, average, and sum up data automatically. The data is retrieved from one table, and the results are shown in another. Pivot Tables make it simple to extract precise data from a vast data set.

Pivot Map

A pivot chart is actually a visual representation of a pivot table. The consumer can have a degree of interactivity with both the data by presenting a visual representation of the pivot table data.

A pivot area is indeed a point upon on worksheet in which you can drag a Pivot Grid field to reorganize the way a report is presented.

The information used to build your pivot table is known as source data. It may come from the worksheet itself or an external database.

Values Area

Value areas are the cells in such a pivot table that contain summary data.

Item

In your pivot table, these are sub-categories of fields. If you have a State area, the values may be Alabama, Alaska, and so on.

Worksheet

Worksheets are papers that are included inside a workbook. Workbooks, commonly known as spreadsheets, can contain several worksheets. The tabs just at the bottom of the screen will show you whichever of your worksheets you're working on right now. The active worksheet and active sheet are other names for this.

The cell is now a rectangle and block that is contained inside a worksheet. Any information you wish to use in your worksheet should be entered into a cell. Depending on what you want to achieve, cells can be color-coded, show text, numbers, and the results of calculations. A cell that is currently available for editing is known as an active cell.

Columns and Rows

Columns and rows determine the alignment of your cells. The columns are vertically oriented, while the rows are horizontally aligned.

Headings for Columns and Rows

These are all the lettered and numbered grey areas that are just outside columns and rows. When you click on a heading, the entire row/column is selected. The headings may also be used to adjust the row height and column width.

Workspace

A workspace, like worksheets in such a workbook, helps you to access several files at once.

The Ribbon is a portion of command tabs located above the workbook. Behind each tab is a plethora of choices.

The cell reference is just a collection of coordinates that uniquely defines a single cell. It is actually made up of numbers and letters. A5 will, for example, point to a cell at the intersection of column A or row 5.

Range of Cells

A cell range is just a series of cells grouped based on several factors. Excel will specify the set, also known as an array, using a comma (:) between cell references. A1:C1, for example, could tell a formula to looks at any cells in such a box bound by columns A and B and rows 4 and 9, while B4:D9 would inform the method to look at any cells in such a box bordered by columns A and B as well as rows 4 and 9. A 3-D reference is a range that spans several worksheets within the same workbook.

Freeze Panes

Freezing Panes makes it easy to find individual columns or rows on the worksheet to remain visible even while scrolling, like header cells that mark a column.

AutoFill

This feature allows you to copy data to multiple cells with ease.

AutoSum

It features the numbers in your sheet and shows the sum in a cell in your choice.

Merged Cell

A merged cell is formed when two or even more cells are merged.

A template is just a formatted worksheet or worksheet intended to assist users in completing a particular task in Excel. Stock research, method maps, and calendars are examples of this.

Operators are symbols and signs that signify which calculation in an expression must be performed. Operators don't have to be simple mathematical types; they can also be contrast, text concatenation, or reference operators.

A formula is actually a set of instructions that are entered into a cell to generate a value. It must start with an equal sign (=). A math formula, cell references, functions, or an operator may all be examples. An expression is another name for a formula.

The Formula Bar, which is located between both the Ribbon and the workbook, displays the contents of even an active cell. And in the case of equations, the equation bar may display all of the formula's components.

Functions are Excel formulas that have been pre-programmed. They're made to make potentially complicated formulas in such a worksheet easier to understand.

Error Code

If Excel detects a problem with such a formula, an error code appears.

Cell formatting is the process of altering how cell data is represented in a spreadsheet. Just the appearance of cells is altered as they are formatted; the value inside the cells remains unchanged.

Conditional formatting is used when a cell meets certain conditions, such as identical values or values above or below a certain threshold.

Filters are rules which you can use to determine which rows in such a worksheet should be shown. Data like conditions and values may be used in these filters.

Workbook

An Excel spreadsheet document is referred to as a workbook. The workbook stores all of your information and helps you to sort and measure the results. A Shared Workbook is a workbook that several users can access and edit on the same network.

Chapter 2.   Basics of Excel

Since you're just getting started with Spreadsheet, there seem to be a few essential instructions that you should learn. Excel includes stuff like:

- Making a fresh worksheet from the ground up.
- Column content and headers are written and formatted.
- Using a worksheet to do simple calculations such as addition, subtraction, multiplication, and division.
- Excel's fill-in-the-blank functionality.
- In a worksheet, maintain column and row headings showing as you keep scrolling these, so you understand what information you're inputting as you travel down the page.
- Individual columns, rows, and worksheets can be added or removed.

Getting Started with Excel

Whenever you launch Excel, it does not launch with a blank sheet. Rather, you'll be sent to Excel's Main page, where you could load a current worksheet or select a template. For better accessibility, Excel shows worksheets you've previously utilized, bookmarked, or linked to you. If you have any worksheets that you use frequently, you may attach those to this Main page to make them simpler to discover. Select "New worksheet" if you don't use a preexisting style. Let us grab a short glance around it and examine some of its most frequent vocabularies once you're on Excel's primary screen.

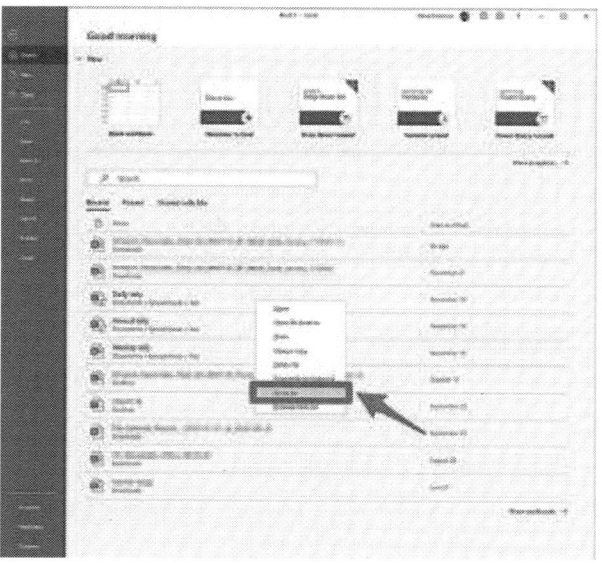

Some Terminologies of Excel

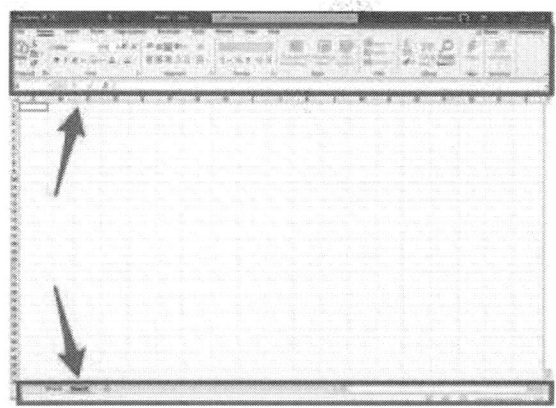

Now let us take a proper glance along and learn a few of the most frequent vocabulary while you're on Excel's primary screen. A notebook is a name given to a Spreadsheet. A notebook is a spreadsheet with one or more pages; by design, a new notebook starts with just one page. Using the extra "+" icon on the main screen will add more spreadsheets to a notebook and shift between pages while using options. Sheets may be closely related to one another, and every Spreadsheet may be titled. Sheet2 can, for instance, perform a computation using data from Sheet4. You'll probably find tools to modify the perspective at the edge of the screen on the right-hand side; for instance, one can get printed copies of the worksheet and then use the zooming scale to modify the scale of the worksheet on your monitor.

You Can also Format the Cells

Whenever it refers to structuring and organizing the contents of cells, Excel is comparable to Word in many aspects. To utilize various editing features such as font, italics, underlining, and font color choices, go to the Menu bar. Textual and cell backdrops can indeed be shaded and colored. Remember that a cell in Spreadsheet is treated as an independent component. One can't arrange distinct numerals, characters, or phrases inside a cell individually, so the bolded text and textual color will be the same. By sliding the top border of a cell, one can modify its dimension. Place the cursor over its separation seen in the middle cells in the column headers at the start of the worksheet if certain cells in a column have data that continues further than the edge of the column and is concealed by data to the side. Then, to expand the full columns, select it.

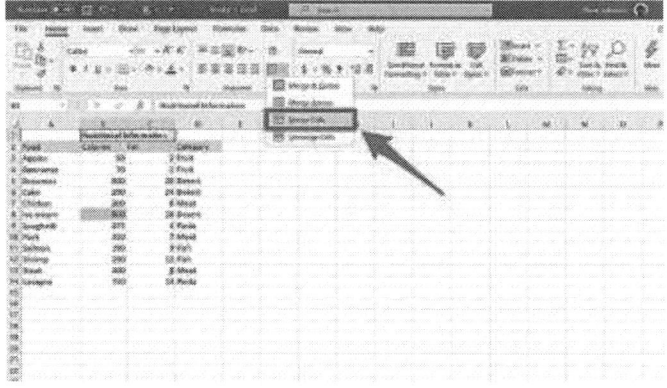

A further option is to reformat the cell so that the word wrap inside this instead of adjusting the cell's dimensions to ensure that the content is viewable. You can also combine multiple cells into the same, which would be useful for designing a column with both words and pictures.

You Can Perform Calculations

Excel is essentially a spreadsheet that allows you to conduct computations utilizing various cells. To combine values in a cell, select the cell, then write "is equal to" this informs Excel that you're typing an equation, and it will attempt to interpret anything that follows as a computation. Then type "3+3+3," click "Submit," and "9" will appear inside the cell. Insert digits in three close cells, including 2,3,4, to combine numerous cells altogether. After that, enter "is equal to" in an individual box, select the very first cell containing numerals, press "plus," and select the next cell. Select the next cell by pressing "plus" once more. When you click "Submit," the cell will convert it into a computation that collectively adds all the selected cells. All fundamental mathematics, like addition, subtraction, multiplying, and dividing, can be used differently.

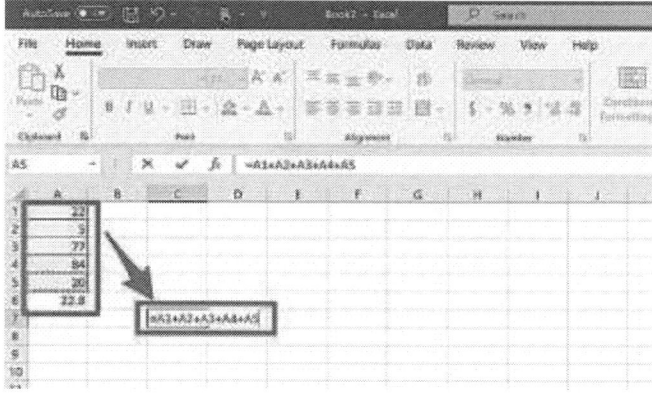

Codes that perform typical processes can also be found in Excel files. Such macros can conduct advanced categorizing and organizing chores and do a range of computations on the given information, but they will be deactivated by design due to safety concerns. Nevertheless, one should first activate macros in Excel if users wish to explore features, so you'll need to activate macros for a worksheet that utilizes them.

Adding a Cell and a Row

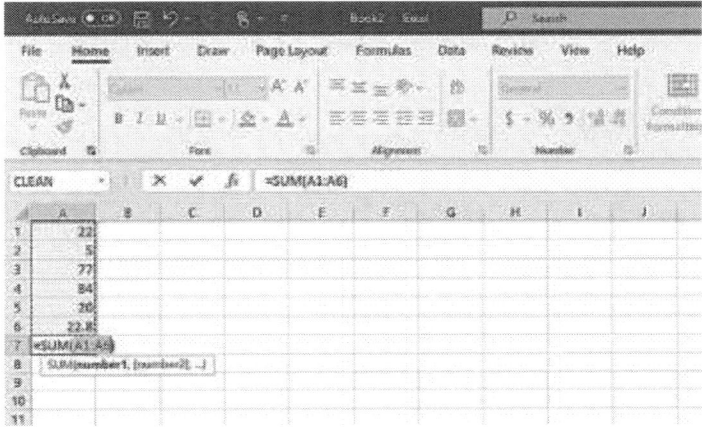

Excel enables basic computations such as combining integers in a column or row simply. Tap in an individual cell beneath the entries you wanted to add if you've got a row of digits and would like to obtain the sum. Please ensure you're on the main page of the interface before pressing the "Add" option. If the full column isn't automatically selected, click and drag the cursor to pick the cells you'd like to include. The amount should show in the cell if you click "Submit." There are numerous methods to combine numbers in a worksheet because it's such a prevalent usage for Excel.

How to Use Formulas in Excel

Although simple computations can be done in this manner, Excel contains thousands of formulae, many familiar and many obscure, which users may use to manipulate the variables in your worksheet. A few of those carry out computations, whereas others provide data on them. You shouldn't have to understand all of them or even all of them, but knowing where and when to look for them and when to use them can come in helpful when the need arises. When you know the title of the equation you would like to employ, enter "is equal to" preceded by the method's initial character in a cell. For instance, if you wish to find the averages of numerous cells, type "is equal to a." All of the equations that start with the initial A will be displayed in an options list. Try spelling "Avera" or navigate downwards until you reach it, then double "AVERAGE." Then either set the data to averaged or choose a type of cell to run the algorithm on.

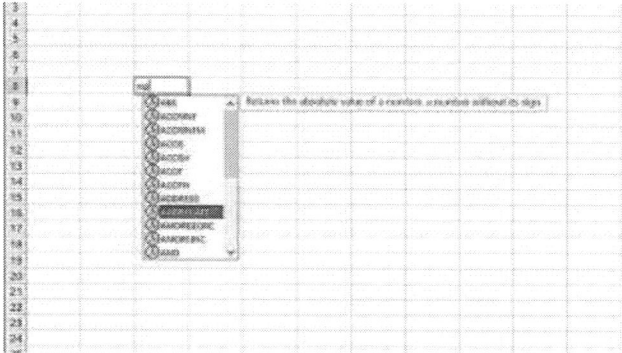

You can also search for equations. Select "Economic," or "Mathematics and Trigonometry" from the "Formulas" menu, and then "AutoSum," "Finance," or "Trigonometry & Addition and subtraction." Then choose the equation you'd like to use. Each equation comes with a thorough help sheet that exhibits signs and describes when to use the method.

You Can also Make a Graph in Excel

The capability to visualize your information by showing it in a graphical form is among Excel's very useful capabilities. More than a hundred graphs are included in Excel, and they may be made almost instantly by picking a set of outcomes and a diagram of the Ribbon. Making a bar graph or a line chart is rather easy, and when you've mastered them, additional diagrams become relatively straightforward as well.

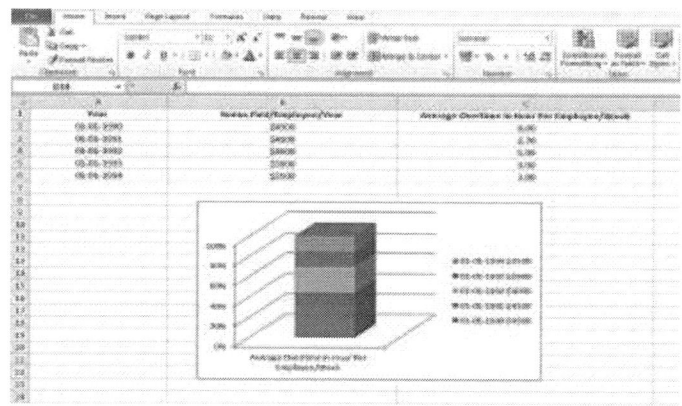

Data Representation via a Pivot Table

Although pivot tables may appear overwhelming, they are simple to design and significantly understand the research in your worksheets. They essentially allow you to "pivot" the way you receive details in a worksheet. Assume you had a spreadsheet that listed the higher calorie content of a range of foods. This Spreadsheet's table format renders it difficult to understand. You may convert this into a table format via an associated pivot chart with just a few taps. In the Spreadsheet with information you wish to visualize, select an empty cell. Now select "PivotTable" from the "Add" option. Pick a type of cell with your cursor that contains the complete collection of data.

The choice will display in the "Make PivotTable" window. "Okay" should be selected. Select two axes to show inside the additional "PivotChart Data" window. Select "meal" and "calls" on this Spreadsheet, for instance, to see tables and charts about how many calories intake in each food item. A pivot table is handy, but it may not provide much more information than the original information. However, suppose you uncheck cuisine but instead correlate calorie intake to food categories. In that case, you could see how every group stacks up in terms of overall calorie intake, as the pivot table and figure add the calorie intake of all the products inside

You Can Add Text, Photos, Graphs and Charts to Improve Your Spreadsheet

Alt-text is a useful resource for recognizing pictures, improving SEO, and assisting vision-disabled customers or anybody else who requires extra aid in recognizing the words of visualizations alongside images. Alt text has been most clearly tied with responsive web design; it may be added to photos in any Microsoft Office project, especially worksheets. In addition, you may attach alt text to any picture or graphics in Excel in two methods: the "Visuals" option on the "Enter" menu.

Although most individuals do not do this regularly, it's a nice choice, particularly if your work will be referred to by anybody who utilizes a visual interface.

Following is how to include alternative text in an Excel worksheet:

- Launch Excel and paste the picture you want into a worksheet.
- Under the options list, select the picture and select "Format alt text" On the hand corner of the screen, the Alt Text window will display.
- To characterize the picture, provide the alt text you would like to use.
- Select the option next to "Label as ornamental" if the picture is unnecessary to comprehending the main worksheet - for instance if it's lines or boxes that have been inserted solely for artistic reasons.
- Close the window or select anything else once you're finished. This alt text would be inserted into your page directly.

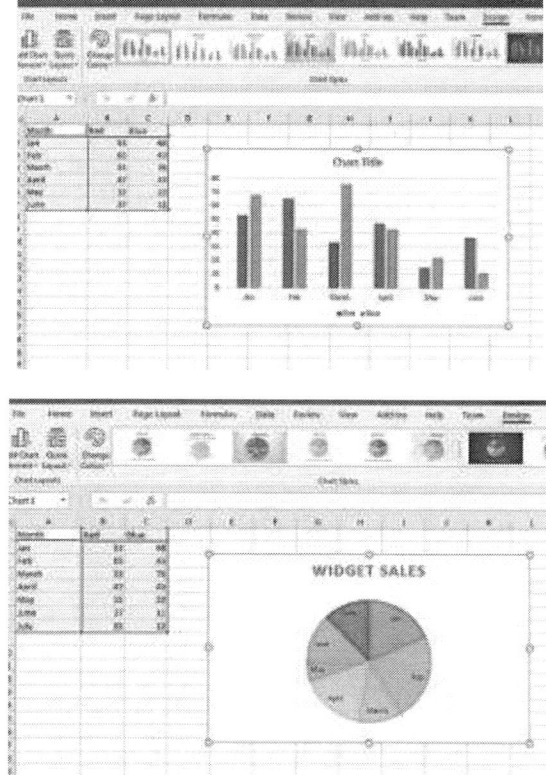

Convert Google Sheets into an Excel Sheet

In many respects, Google sheet and Excel are comparable. Both allow you to construct worksheets for comparable reasons – bills, budgeting, organizing, and hosting parties and they share most of the same capabilities. Even though the tools are extremely identical, some individuals work with Excel rather than Google Sheets. It could also be because you do not need a broadband connection to save your effort, but it could also be that someone is simply comfortable with the system. In any way, you may efficiently translate your files if you began to work on a worksheet with Google Sheets and subsequently desire to utilize Excel.

To do so, use the downloadable features of Google Sheets present on both Mac or Pc.

Following is how to put things to good advantage.

- Click the Sheets worksheet you would like to transfer on either Mac or Pc.
- Select "Files," then hovering over the "Save" button in the drop-down list.
- Select "Excel" from the new option that emerges. By doing so will change the worksheet's layout to Excel. The files would download immediately, or you'll be requested wherever you want it out based on your chrome browser.
- One can launch the new Excel spreadsheet in Excel just like every other Excel document once it is installed.

Use Filters to Make Work Easier

While working with very big information files, it is rarely necessary to simultaneously examine every vertically stacked row. On occasions, you may choose to examine only information that meets specific requirements. That is when filters enter the picture. Filtration enables you to pinpoint your information so that you only see specific rows at the moment. Each row in your information may be filtered in Excel, and after that, you would like whichever cells to see simultaneously. Consider the following example. When choosing the Information box and choosing "Filtering," you may insert a filter. By selecting the button beside the columns, you may specify which of your information should be sorted, increasing or decreasing or displaying individual rows. In the Hogwarts example, suppose that the user wants to view Slytherin pupils. The other rows vanish when the Slytherin filter is applied.

Copy/Paste a Formula

Excel may be launched from either a MacBook or a Windows. You also could discover the program on your Macintosh by launching the Finder app, choosing "Apps" from the menu icon, and afterward choosing "Excel."

- Choose a previously created worksheet or begin a fresh one.
- Click the button containing the equation.
- Twice tap the formula in the equation menu bar to choose it.
- Press "cmd" Plus "C" on one Macbook or "Control" + "C" on one's PC to duplicate the equation. You also can pick "Update" then "Clone" from the menu bar. The equation will be saved to the notepad at this point.

- To transfer the code, select the worksheet wherever you wish to put it. We'll put the equation on a spreadsheet in the current Spreadsheet in this instance.
- Choose the cell in which you wish the equation to appear.
- Press "Cmd" + "V" on one Macbook or "Control" + "V" on one's Windows computer, or choose "Update" then "Transfer" from the main menu.
- To use the equation, press "Access" on one's keypad.

Eliminate Redundant Datasets

Greater databases frequently contain duplicated information. You might have had a collection of many connections within a firm and wish to view simply the total number of firms. In the circumstances like this, deleting redundancies is beneficial. To delete duplication, choose the column that contains multiple copies. Then, click "Delete Multiple copies" from the Information column. A pop-up window will open to verify the information in which you prefer to operate. Simply select "Delete Multiple copies," and you're done.

Additionally, you may use this functionality to delete a whole row depending on the existence of a duplicated column values. Therefore, if you have three rows containing data about Hogwarts but only want to see one, you can pick the entire database and then delete copies depending on the mail. Your resultant collection will contain only unusual identifiers.

Converting the Rows and Columns

Whenever we're working on excel, there are some times where we want to convert columns into rows and rows into columns. This is known as transpose. It would actually take a lot of effort to copy-paste data from a row into a column and not be effective. So here, one can select the transpose option, and within no time, rows will be converted into columns and columns into rows. To begin, select the columns into rows that you wish to rearrange. Choose "Clone" from the context menu of the right-clicked item. Following that, choose the cell in your worksheet wherever you wish to start your initial row or column. Choose "Paste Custom" from the context menu after right-clicking on the cell. A component will emerge; towards the end, you'll see a transposition choice. Choose that checkbox and click OK. The columns have been converted to a row or vise - versa.

You Can also Divide the Data from One Cell to the Other

What about if users wish to divide data contained in a single cell into two distinct cells? For instance, suppose you wish to determine a person's firm name based on their email id. Alternatively, you may wish to divide a person's whole identity into the same first and last surname for use in your email campaign designs. Both are feasible, owing to Spreadsheet. To begin, select the columns you wish to separate. Following that, navigate to the Information menu and choose "Content to Column." A section with extra details will emerge.

- To begin, choose between "Delimited" and "Set Size."
- The term "delimited" refers to the desire to segment the columns using symbols such as parentheses, periods, or spaces.
- "Set Size" indicates that you'd like to specify the precise place of the divide across all sections.
- We'll choose "Delimited" to divide the complete address into first and last names in the scenario.
- Following that, it's important to select the Delimiters. It could be a bar, a semi-colon, a stop, or a gap.
- Once you're satisfied with the display, click "Continue." If you like, this screen will enable you to pick Additional Templates. When finished, click "Next."

Use Formulas to Save Time

Along with performing rather sophisticated computations, Excel can assist you in performing fundamental mathematical operations such as addition, subtraction, multiplication, or division of any of your information.

- Add the Asterisk symbol to multiply.
- Add the - symbol to subtract.
- Insert the Plus symbol to add.
- The Slash symbol is used to divide.

Additionally, you may utilize parentheses to guarantee that particular computations are performed first. For example, the first and second tens were added in the following scenario (1+1*2) when multiplied by the second and third tens.

Change the Color of the Cells by Using Conditional Formatting

It enables you to alter the color of a cell depends on the contents of the cell. For instance, if you'd like to highlight particular values far above normal or in the bottom 15% of your worksheet's information, you may do so. You may use Excel to color similarities across distinct rows. This enables you to access data that is relevant to you rapidly. To begin, choose the collection of cells on which you wish to apply conditional logic. Finally, pick

"Conditional Format" from the Main option and then pick your reasoning from the selection. (You may also write your custom regulation if you like.) A box will appear asking for further details regarding your styling rule. Once you're finished, click "Finish," and your findings should show immediately.

Use of IF logic in Excel

Occasionally, we may not wish to quantify the occurrences of a variable. Rather than that, we want to enter different data into a cell if a matching cell contains that data. For instance, in this scenario, we'd like to offer a higher score to anyone a member of the Slytherin family. So, rather than simply inputting tens next to each Slytherin named person, we may use the IF-THEN Xls equation to indicate that the individual must receive ten points if they are in Slytherin.

The following equation: IF(logical test, true or false value)

Logical Test: The rational check is included within the "IF" clause of the sentence. In this example, Slytherin is used as we wish to ensure that the cell relating to the individual has the word "Slytherin." Make certain to include the quote marks around Slytherin.

Value if True: We'd like to display the value in the cell if the statement is positive. In this example, we would like the cell to contain "10" to signify that the individual received the ten points. Use quote marks if only you wish for the outcome to be text rather than numeric.

Value if False: That's the value we would like the cell to display if the result is negative. In this example, we would like the cell to display "0" to indicate that the individual is not a member of Slytherin. Use quote marks only if you wish for the outcome to be text rather than a statistic.

Chapter 3. Excel Worksheet Operations

Inserting Columns and Rows

You will see the Insert Options button if you insert a row, column, or cell into a worksheet that has been formatted. You will be presented with a list of options pertaining to how the inserted row or column should be formatted. Below is a summary of those options.

The format is the same as above.

- The new row is formatted according to the row above the inserted row.

The format is the same as below.

- The new row is formatted the same as the row below the inserted row.

Same as on the left

- The new column is formatted in the same way as the column to the left of the inserted column.

The same format as the right.

- The new column is formatted in the same manner as the column to the right of the inserted column.

Formatting; simple formatting

New rows and columns are formatted according to the default.

To add a column

- Select Insert from the right-click menu of a column header.

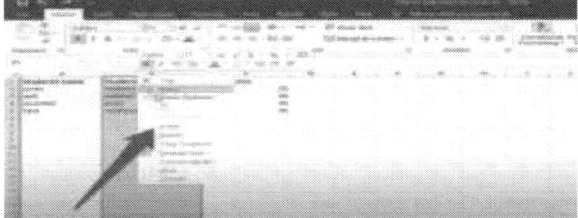

To insert multiple columns into

- Insert the same number of columns as the number of column headers you selected.
- Choose Insert from the context menu by right-clicking any column header.

To insert a row:

- Select Insert from the right-click menu of a row header.

To insert multiple rows:

- Insert a row header for each number of rows you wish to insert.
- Select any row header, then choose Insert from the right-click menu.

Deleting Columns and Rows

To remove one or more columns, click the Delete button.

- To delete a column, select its header.
- Right-click and then select "Delete."

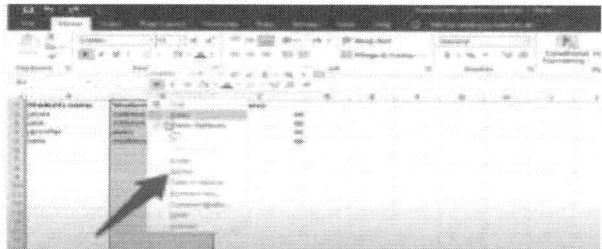

To delete one or more rows:

- If you want to delete rows, select their headers.
- Right-click and then select "Delete."

Clear a Cell's Contents

Cells can be cleared to remove the contents (formulas and data), formats (such as number formats, conditional formats, and borders), and any comments that appear in the document. The cleared cells appear as blank or unformatted placeholders during the spreadsheet processing.

To clear a cell's content:

- Select the particular cells, rows, or columns that you actually want to clear.

- Choose one of the following from the Editing group on the Home tab:
- Click on "Clear All" to remove all contents, formats, and comments from the selected cells.
- By clicking Clear Formats, you will only remove the formats that were applied to the selected cells.

- Clear the contents of only the selected cells and leave any formats and comments untouched by clicking Clear Contents.
- Click Clear Comments and Notes to delete any comments or notes attached to the selected cells.
- Select Clear Hyperlinks to remove any hyperlinks attached to selected cells.

Notes:

- Using the delete or backspace keys, you actually can delete a cell's contents without removing the cell format or the cell comment.
- Clearing a cell with Clear All or Clear Contents removes the value from the cell, so any formula referring to that cell receives a value of 0 (zero).
- You can select the cells and delete them if you want to remove them from the worksheet and reposition the surrounding cells to fill the space. You can delete cells in the Cells group on the Home tab by clicking the arrow next to Delete.

Cut or Copy Data

You can move or copy the contents of cells using Cut, Copy, and Paste. Additionally, you can copy specific attributes or contents from cells. The resulting value of a formula can be copied without copying the formula, or the formula can be copied only.

The formulas and values in a cell, as well as the cell formatting and comments, are moved or copied when you move or copy a cell.

With Excel, you can move cells by dragging them to another location or by cutting and pasting them.

Move Cells by Dragging and Dropping

You can move or copy individual cells or ranges of cells.

- Place the cursor at the selection's edge.
- Drag the pointer to move the cell or range of cells when the move pointer appears.

Move cells by using Cut and Paste

- Make a selection of one or more cells.
- Click Home > Cut or press Ctrl + X.

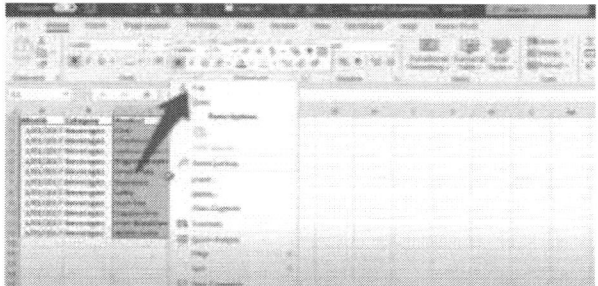

- Choose the cell where the data should be moved.
- Click Home > Paste or press Ctrl + V.

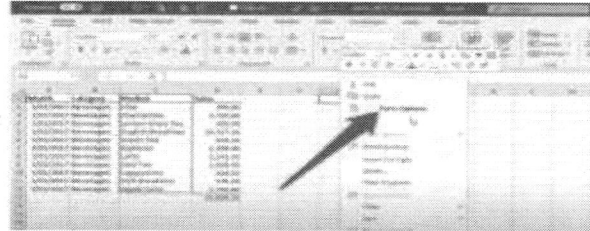

You can copy and paste cells in your worksheet with the use of the Copy and Paste commands.

- Cells or ranges of cells should be selected.
- Click "Copy" or press "Ctrl + C."

- Ctrl + V or Ctrl + V are shortcuts for Paste.

Copy or move just the Contents of the Cell

- Click twice on the cell containing the data you want to move or copy.
- Double-clicking the cell gives you the option to edit and select the data directly, but you can also edit and select it in the formula bar.
- Click on the characters you would wish to copy or move in the cell.

How to Select Cells or Ranges

Do one of the following list in the Clipboard group on the Home tab:

- The selection can be moved by clicking "Cut."
- The shortcut key is Ctrl+X.
- Click Copy to copy the selection.
- Alternatively, you can press Ctrl+C.
- Select where in the cell you would like to paste the characters or double-click another cell to copy or move the data.
- Choose the Clipboard group from the Home tab, and click Paste.
- You can actually also use the Ctrl+V keyboard shortcut.
- Click enter

Preview an Item Before Pasting

Have you ever been disappointed that the content you copied and pasted didn't turn out the way you wanted it to? When you copy and paste content between Office applications, you can preview how it will look using the new Live Preview function.

Not all paste preview options will be available in every case. You will have options depending on which applications you use and what content you copy.

- Right-click and select Copy, press Ctrl + C, or select Copy from the Home tab to copy your content.
- Next, choose where you'd like to paste the content. Paste Preview buttons can now be accessed either from the Paste dropdown list on the Home tab or by right-clicking.
- By hovering your mouse over each Paste Options button, you can see a preview of what it would look like when you paste it.
- Find the paste option you like and click the corresponding button.
- By clicking "Paste," the entire document will be pasted with all its formatting.

- The values will be pasted as they are, without formatting, and if formatting is used, only formatting will be pasted, without values. Move your mouse over Paste Special to see if there are any additional paste options.

Paste Special

In Microsoft Office applications such as Access, Word, PowerPoint, Excel, and Outlook, you can specify formatting when pasting slides, text, pictures, objects, and tables from another program or the web.

Similar to pictures and other objects in a presentation, the text has its own formatting, such as typeface, color, and font size. In Microsoft Office programs like PowerPoint or Word, when you copy text with different formatting, the text is automatically reformatted to match the formatting of the text where it is being pasted. It is actually possible to retain the original formatting by using Paste Special or by pasting it as a link or a picture, for example.

- Copy or cut the slides, pictures, texts, or objects that you wish to paste.
- To insert that item, click the appropriate location in your office file.

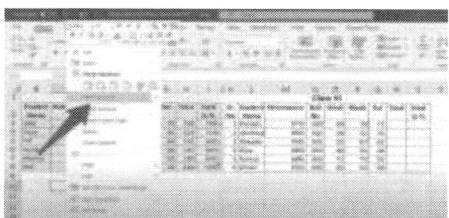

- Choose the option you would like to use under Paste Special by clicking the arrow under the Clipboard group on the Home tab.

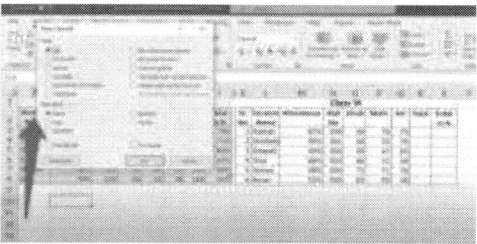

Settings for Formulas

For as long as modern computing has existed, Microsoft Excel has been one of the most important tools. More than a million people use Microsoft Excel spreadsheets every day for managing projects, tracking finances, creating charts and graphs, and even balancing their time.

A spreadsheet program calculates values by using mathematical formulas and data in cells, unlike other applications like Word. Occasionally, however, Excel formulas do not work correctly.

In most cases, people accidentally activate the "Show Formulas" button. When this is active, the applied formulas won't work. Click on the Formulas tab to find this setting. When pressed, the button displays the formula rather than the result, which is intended for auditing formulas. It may help if you turn it off if you previously turned it on.

Here's how to do it:

Click on the Show Formulas button under the Formula Tab > Formula Auditing Group.

Your Excel calculation option may be set to manual instead of automatic if you cannot update the value you've entered.

You can fix this by changing the calculation mode from manual to automatic.

- Go to the spreadsheet that's causing you difficulties.
- You can then navigate to the Formulas tab and select Calculation from there.
- In the Calculation Options dropdown, select Automatic.

If you prefer, you can change the calculation options within Excel.

In the top left corner, click Office > Excel options > Formulas > Workbook Calculation > Automatic

Deleting Data and the Undo Command

Using either the delete key or the clear button on the ribbon is the most common way to remove data from a computer. Alternatively, you can also delete rows, columns, or cells to remove data.

Let's have a look now.

Using the Clear button on the home ribbon in Excel is one way to remove data.

- Select "Clear Contents" if you only wish to remove data.
- Select "Clear All" to remove both the contents and the formatting.

The delete key is a faster way to clear content. By selecting the cells, then pressing the delete key, you can delete them.

The deletion of cells in this manner does not remove the formatting but removes the data. If you actually would also like to remove the formatting, use "Clear all" in the Clear section of the Home ribbon.

Alternatively, you can delete entire rows or columns in a worksheet to remove data.

Simply select the rows or columns containing the data you wish to remove and delete them using one of the methods as discussed earlier.

You can actually use this method to clean up a worksheet quickly by removing all data and formatting.

- In addition, you can right-click and select "Delete" from the context menu.
- Once the Delete dialog box appears, you can select an appropriate option.

It is always a good idea to keep in mind other data that may exist elsewhere in the worksheet when deleting rows or columns.

If you have entered data in error and you don't want to go through the stress of having to keep pressing the backspace or delete key, you can

Simply press Ctrl+Z. This will undo whatever mistake that must have been made.

Adjusting Columns and Rows

Cells can be inserted into a worksheet in the same way as rows and columns. In a column, you can use the Insert dialog box to shift the cells around the inserted cells down (in a row) or to the right (in a column).

Select the cells you want to move and point to the selection's border to move the data. Upon changing to a four-pointed arrow, you can drag selected cells to the target location on the worksheet.

Excel displays a dialog box when it detects that the destination cells contain data, asking if you want to overwrite them. This can be done by overwriting the data or by canceling the move.

In order to change the height of the rows

- Resize rows by selecting their headers.
- Choose a row header and click the bottom border.
- As soon as the pointer changes into a vertical arrow, drag the border to adjust the row's height.

Or

- Resize rows by selecting their headers.
- Right-click the selected row header, and then choose Row Height.
- Enter a new row height in the Row Height dialog box.
- Click the OK button.

To change the column width

- Select the headers to resize the columns.
- Point the cursor to the right border of a selected column header.
- Once a double-headed horizontal arrow appears, drag the border of the column until the desired width is reached.

Or

- Column headers for the columns you would like to resize should be selected.
- To change the column width, right-click any of the selected column headers.

- Fill out the Column Width dialog box with a new width for the columns you selected.
- Click OK.

Find and Replace

Find and Replace is a useful feature of Excel that is often overlooked.

Find and Replace Text and Numbers in Excel

Having to look for a specific value in a large spreadsheet is a common task. Fortunately, this is made easy using Find and Replace.

If you want to search the entire worksheet

- Click any cell or choose the column or range of cells you want to analyze.
- Select Home > Find & Select > Find or press the Ctrl + F keyboard shortcut.
- Enter the text or number you are looking for in the "Find What" text box.

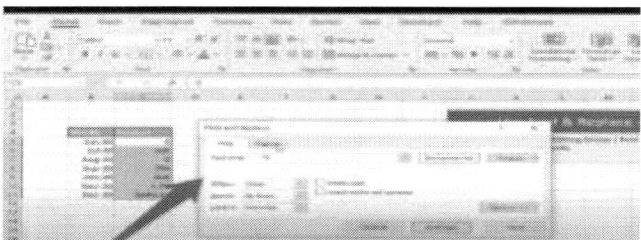

- Click on "Find Next" to find the first instance of a value in the search area; click "Find Next" again to find the second instance, and so on.
- By selecting "Find All", you will see all instances of the value along with information such as the book, sheet, and cell where it appears.
- Click on an item to be taken to that cell.

It can be useful to find specific or all instances of a value within a spreadsheet to save time browsing through them.

- For any occurrences of a value that you want to replace
- Select "Replace" from the menu.

- Enter the text you wish to replace or the number within the "Replace With" text box.

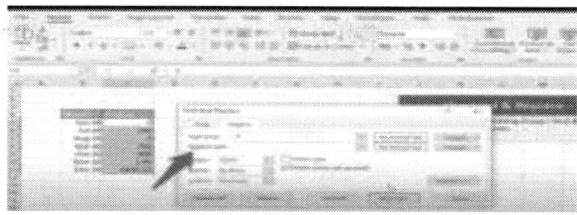

- Click "Replace" to modify each occurrence individually, or choose "Replace All" to modify all occurrences simultaneously.

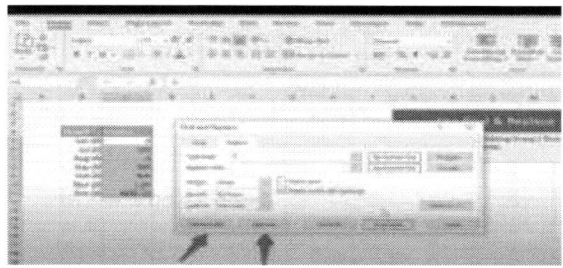

- Values should be formatted differently

The formatting of values can also be found and replaced.

You can pick a range of cells to search for and replace, or you can click on any cell on the worksheet to search the entire active worksheet.

- Select Home > Find and Replace then click on Replace to display the Find and Replace window.
- Simply click the "Options" button to view the Find and Replace options.

For finding and replacing text or numbers, you do not need to enter them.

Simply click the "Format" button beside the "Find What" and "Replace With" fields to format them.

If you would like to replace or find a particular format, specify it. A preview of the actual format appears in the Find and Replace window. displays a preview of the formatting.

You may also set any additional options you wish, then click "Replace All" to change all locations in which the formatting is used.

Sorting

The sorting of data is an important part of data analysis. It would be useful to arrange a list of names alphabetically, compile a list of inventory levels from highest to lowest, or organize rows by color or icon. Organizing and finding the right data can help you quickly visualize and understand data, make better decisions, and ultimately make sense of your data.

The data can be sorted by text (A to Z or Z to A), by numbers (smallest to largest or largest to smallest), and by dates (oldest to newest and newest to oldest). A custom list can also be sorted by size (for instance, large, medium, or small) or by formats, such as font color, cell color, or icon set.

Sort text

1. Sort the column by selecting a cell.
    - In order to quickly sort in ascending order, click Sort A to Z.
    - Sort quickly into descending order by clicking "Sort Z to A."

Potential Problems

- Verify that text is being stored for all data. You must format numbers or text in a column that contains both numbers and text. If this format is not applied, the numbers stored as numbers are sorted before the numbers stored as text. For formatting selected data as text, Press Ctrl+1 to launch the Format Cells dialog, select the Number tab, then choose General, Number, or Text under Category.
- Any leading spaces should be removed. Sometimes, data imported from another application will have leading spaces inserted before the data. Get rid of the leading spaces before sorting the data. The TRIM function can be used to do this, or you can do it manually.

Sort Numbers

1. Sort the column by selecting a cell.
2. Go to the option Data tab, in the Sort & Filter group, do one of the following:
    - You can sort from lowest to highest by clicking on "Sort From Smallest to Largest."
    - You can sort larger items into smaller ones by clicking "Sort by largest to smallest."

Dates of Times Sorted

1. Sort the column by selecting a cell.
2. Go to the option Data tab, in the Sort & Filter group, do one of the following:
   - To sort from actually an earlier to a later date or time, click Sort Oldest to Newest.
   - To sort from a later date or time to an earlier date or time, click Sort Newest to Oldest.

Note:

- If the results are actually not what you expected, check that dates and times are stored as dates and times; otherwise, there may be text stored in the column. A column of dates and times must be formatted as a date or time serial number for Excel to sort them correctly. Dates and times that Excel cannot identify as dates or times are stored as text instead.

For sorting by days of the week, format the cells by weekday. When sorting by weekday regardless of the date, convert the cells to text with the TEXT function. TEXT, on the other hand, returns text values, so the sorting operation would rely on alphanumeric data.

Sort more than one column or row at a time.

It may be necessary to sort more than one column or row when you have data that you want to group by the same value in one row or column before sorting the next row or column in the group of equal values. You can, for example, sort by department first (to group all the employees in the same department together) and then by name (to alphabetize the names within a department).There are up to 64 columns available for sorting.

Select any cell in the data range.

Choose Sort from the Sort & Filter group on the Data tab.

Select the first column that you actually want to sort in the Sort by section of the Sort dialog box.

The sort type can be selected under Sort On. You can do either of the following:

- Sort by using text, number, or date and time by selecting Values.
- If you want to sort by format, select Cell Color, Font Color, or Cell Icon.

Under Order, select how you want the list sorted. You can select from the following options:

- When choosing text values, choose from A to Z or Z to A.
- When comparing numbers, choose Smallest to Largest or Largest to Smallest.
- For date or time values, choose "Oldest to Newest" or "Newest to Oldest."
- Select Custom Lists to sort based on the list you have created.
- Click Add Level to add another column to sort by, then repeat steps three through five.
- If you would like to copy a column to sort by, select it and click Copy Level.
- The column to sort by can be deleted by selecting it and then clicking Delete Level.
- The order of the columns can actually be changed by selecting an entry and clicking the Up or Down arrow next to the Options button.
- The higher entry in the list is sorted before the lower entry.

Sort by cell color, font color, or icon.

A table column or a range of cells can also be sorted by the color of the cell or the color of the font if those colors have been manually or conditionally formatted. A conditional formatting icon set can also be used for sorting.

- Pick a cell in the column that you wish to sort.
- Go to the Data tab, in the Sort & Filter group, select Sort.
- Select the column you want to sort in the Sort by field under Column in the Sort Dialog Box.
- Click Sort On, then select Cell Color, Font Color, or Cell Icon.
- In the Order section, click the arrow next to the button and then select a cell color, font color, or cell icon, depending on the type of format you want.
- Then, select the sorting method. Choose from the following options:

0. To move the color of a cell, the font color, or the icon to the top or left, choose "On Top" or "On Left," respectively, in a column sort.

1. If you wish to move the cell color, font color, or icon to the bottom or right of a column, or the right of a row, select On Bottom.

- Click Add Level, then repeat steps three through five to specify the next cell color, font color, or icon to sort by.

Then, the "by" box should be populated with the same column, and the order should be the same.

Repeat for every other cell color, font color, or icon you want to include in the sort.

Sort by a custom list

Custom lists can be used to sort in a user-defined order. You might actually want to sort a column by its values, such as high, medium, and low. You want rows with "high" to appear first, then "medium," and finally "low." What can you do? An alphabetical sort would put "high" at the top, while "low" comes before "medium." In the case of sorting "Z to A," medium would be at the top, and low would be in the middle. No matter which orders you choose, make sure that "Medium" is in the middle. If you create your own list, you can circumvent this problem.

Alternatively, create your own list:

- Enter the values you wish to sort by in a range of cells, from top to bottom, in the order that you desire.
- You can now select the range that you entered.
- Navigate to File > Options > Advanced > General > Edit Custom Lists, then click Import in the Custom Lists dialog box, and then click on the OK button twice.
- Sort the cells in the column you selected.
- Select Sort from the Sort & Filter group on the Data tab.
- Select the column that you want to sort by in the "Sort by" or "Then by" box of the Sort dialog box.
- Go to Order and choose "Custom List."
- Select the list that you want to view in the Custom Lists dialog box. You should now click "High," "Medium, or "Low on the custom list you created.
- Select OK.

Chapter 4. Getting to Know Formulas

Formulas are the heart of Excel. You should learn how to write formulas that do calculations, combine values, and refer to cells in your spreadsheet.

Types of Formulas

Excel provides three types of calculation formulas: arithmetic, financial, and look-up. Each of these formulas is defined with a particular function key.

Arithmetic Formulas

Arithmetic formulas are used to perform calculations and determine the results of mathematical operations with numbers. The most common arithmetic formulas you will use in Excel are simple math functions and common arithmetic operators (such as +, -, *, /). You can also find these functions in your word processor's calculator.

Financial Formulas

Financial formulas calculate financial transactions using money values, such as interest rates and percentages. To learn how to write financial formulas in Excel, you will need to know how to use some financial formulas in formulas that operate with these values.

Look-Up Formulas

Look-up formulas are used to find information, such as the size or year of a company's financial statement or the cost of gasoline in 5 different states. The most common look-up formulas you will use in Excel are INDEX, MATCH, and IFERROR. These functions determine the results of locating data in a range or table.

How to Work with Formulas

You can place a formula into a cell by typing it or by copying it from another cell. These steps will show you how to enter data in a cell, including entering formulas.

1. Enter data in a cell by typing.
2. To enter a formula, click in the cell, and then type = (equal sign).
3. In the formula bar, type the formula's components (arguments), such as values and operators.
4. Press "Enter" to finish.
5. To see your formula result in the cell, go to the cell and click "Formula." The Formula bar displays your formula and its result.

Before you learn how to write formulas, you should be aware of the following things:

Defining Functions in Excel

A function is actually a set of instructions that performs a calculation or an action on the values in a cell. The formula enclosed in parentheses is called an argument. A function can obtain any number of arguments, but the number and types of these arguments depend on the function.

In Excel, you can create two types of functions: User-defined (formulas) and built-in (built-in functions).

User-Defined Functions

A user-defined function is a piece of programming code that you create. You write the code in Visual Basic for Applications (VBA), which is the programming language for Excel and other Office applications. Then, you run the VBA macro to see the results of your function in the worksheet.

Built-In Functions

Built-in functions are formulas that come with Excel and perform a variety of actions on cells. Most of them are simple mathematical formulas, but some of them perform more complex tasks, such as looking up data in a table.

Built-in functions have the following characteristics:

- They can be used in any worksheet.
- They are easy to use and understand.
- They are portable from one workbook to another.
- They have "built-in" error checking, so if you make an error in your function, Excel displays an alert dialog box and stops executing the function.
- You cannot create any new built-in functions in Excel. You can only use the ones that are available or add them to a custom toolbar later.
- They are named by the first letters of the function.
- They generally perform the same actions in all Excel versions.
- They use a set of arguments that you specify and may have functions that return values.
- Depending on the type of function, you can use one or more arguments.

Understanding Arguments

The arguments for a function are the values you put inside the parentheses in a formula. The arguments are used by the function to calculate its results. You must specify all the required arguments when you create a function, but you can usually leave empty any optional arguments that you do not need.

Example of arguments:

=sum(A1:B10)

=Sum(Number1, ...)

In the formula above, the arguments are used as follows:

Number1 - this argument is the input range, which can be an array formula. For example, if you want to sum cells A1 through A10, you will input =sum(A1:A10). These arguments are the other input ranges for your formula.

The output will be a single cell with the value of each range (the sum of column C) added together (sum of B column).

=Date(year,month,date)

In the formula above, the first argument is the date to find, and the second argument is the year, month, and date.

=FV(rate, nper, pmt, pv, [fnce])

In the formula above, the following arguments are specified: rate — this argument is used to set the interest rate for this payment. nper — this argument sets the number of payments. pmt — this argument is used to set the amount of each payment. pv —this argument sets the current unpaid balance. [fnce] – if you do not specify an optional argument, you must use brackets ([]) to indicate that it is an optional one.

=if(logical_test,value_if_true,[value_if_false])

In the formula above, the following arguments are:

x: The result of the logical test can be either "true" or "false."

value_if_x: The value the formula returns when the variable x is true. If it evaluates to false, then that argument will not appear in the formula.

#N/A: This means that there is no such value for this argument.

Reasons for Using Formulas in Excel

There are various reasons why you will use formulas in Excel. The first reason is that doing so enables you to see the results of a calculation or an action on your worksheet. This can help you make better-informed decisions and control the actions in your worksheet.

The second reason is that you might want to perform calculations with variables, such as the number of sales or the daily sales so that you can change these numbers without having to change all your formulas.

The third reason is that performing calculations can help you manage multiple worksheets in a workbook. For instance, in a business bookkeeping application, you might need to enter data for your vendors, customers, and employees. If you do this in one worksheet, you need to check and update that data in all the other worksheets. By using functions, you can easily update those values after entering data into the first worksheet, and all the other customer, sales, and employee records will be updated automatically.

The fourth reason is if you want to make up your own functions by using a variety of Excel features by combining different parts of Excel. For example, you can form an Excel formula to perform a calculation on the New Year's date and to create a custom date field in your worksheet.

The fifth reason is that even if you do not use formulas in Excel, every time you save your workbook, the workbook displays formulas and comments, which are helpful for program writers and document maintainers.

Important Things to Know About Functions

There are five important things that I want to share with you:

1. Functions can be very long, so be careful about what you enter in the cell. The function enclosed in parentheses is called the function's argument or argument. For example, the formula =COUNTA(A:B:D) refers to the range A:B:D.
2. Functions can also include text (words). If you actually select a cell that contains the formula and then copy it to another cell, Excel pastes that text instead of replacing it with numbers within the formula.
3. If you create a formula with incorrect spelling or syntax, Excel displays a #NAME? error in the cell. The formula works only when you correct the error.

4. The question mark (?) is called a wildcard because it represents any value. When Excel replaces the question mark with a value, it performs calculations on that value according to what you specified in your function formula.
5. If you press F4 on a cell that contains a formula, Excel displays the results of your function and its arguments. This is called "displaying the formula." You can also press F4 to display information about your function in the formula bar.

Chapter 5. Excel Formulas and Functions

Mathematics is not new in our world of today as calculations is what we do always. With Excel formulas and functions, calculations are made easy. There are many helpful formulas and functions integrated into Microsoft Excel by its developer, and that makes things easy and time saving. You do not need to start counting numbers with your fingers. Just know the formula to enter in the spreadsheet you are working on, and you will have the answer right there before you. That is what this part will teach you; knowing the formulas or functions to type in a spreadsheet to arrive at a particular answer. I will start from the simple formulas and functions, and then progress to the complex ones.

I want to bring something to your notice, before you can perform any calculation in Excel, first introduce = sign before you can continue. Introduction of that "=" sign informs Excel program that it is calculation you want to make.

Addition in Excel Spreadsheet

There are ways you can add values in Excel spreadsheet. These as just simple Arithmetic that you can complete so easily but if you do not understand how to get it done, it becomes a problem. I will walk you through on how to add numbers in Excel spreadsheet using sample data.

Data for sum calculation in Excel

Using the data above, if I want to add the numbers, I will first select the cell where I want to have the answer of my addition. The next step is to sum the entire numbers by typing =1+4+9+8+6+3 and then press the Enter key of my computer keyboard.

Photo shows the inserted addition formula in a cell

On hitting the Enter key, you will see the answer to the typed numbers appear.

There is another way to sum numbers in Excel. This approach involves entering the cells number instead of the values. For instance, referring to the data sample I initially uploaded, the value "8" is in cell B1. So, I can use the cell identity to add rather than the value it contains and still get the same answer at the end. To get that done, select the cell where you want to have your answer inserted. On doing this, the answer to the summation gets inserted in the initially selected cell.

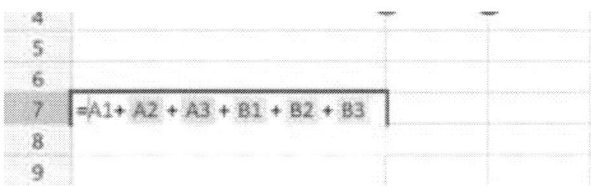

Addition using cell identity

The photo above is how I added the numbers using the individual cells identity.

Summing Values in Many Cells at Once

What of a situation where you have many numbers in many cells of your spreadsheet and you want to add them once? Will you be using the 2 approaches I explained? Using any of the two methods I just explained will be timing consuming. As I result of that, I will walk you through on how you can add many numbers in different cells as fast as possible. I will be using a new sample data for the explanation.

Sample data for the new addition

If I want to sum the above numbers as fast as possible, the first step to take is to select the cell I want to have the answer by just a click on it. The next step is to type =SUM(and then highlight all the cells with the numbers I want to sum, and then close the parenthesis with) and lastly press the Enter keyboard. As soon as you do that, the entire numbers become summed and you then see the answer in the initially selected cell.

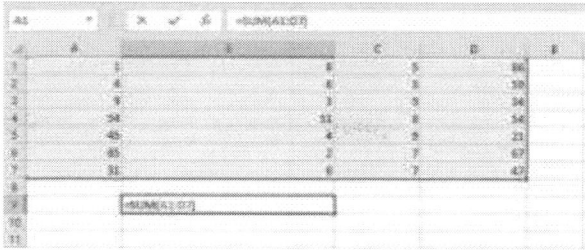

The way to sum many numbers as it appears in a cell

Subtraction in Excel

Another common Mathematics task done in spreadsheet is subtraction. You can subtract one value from the other.

Let me assume you are a businessman or woman that buys and sell some products. Sometimes after making sales, you can use formula in Excel to determine your profit. The data below is what I will use to explain my point practically.

	A	B	C	D
1	COST PRICE ($)	SELLING PRICE ($)	PROFIT ($)	
2	12000	12300		
3				
4				
5				

Data for subtraction calculation

Going with the data above, if I want to subtract the cost price from the selling to get profit, the first step to take is to select the cell where I want to have the answer for my calculation. Then, I will type =B2-A2 and press the Enter key of my computer keyboard. On doing this, the answer to the calculation will be inserted in the cell.

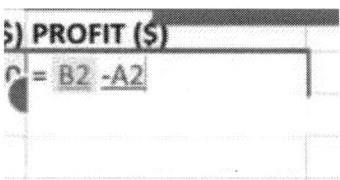

The typed subtraction formula in a cell

There is another method to carryout subtraction in Excel spreadsheet. This is directly typing the values. Going with my sample information for this subtraction teaching, I will type =12300-12000 in the cell where I want to have my answer and hit the Enter key of my computer keyboard. This will give me the correct answer to the command immediately.

Exercise on Subtraction

Using the correct formula, find the profit made in the business using the data displayed below.

	A	B	C
1	COST PRICE ($)	SELLING PRICE ($)	PROFIT ($)
2	200	220	
3			
4			
5			
6			

Data to be used for the exercise

Finding Average

With Excel, you can find the average of some numbers. Excel is developed in a way that once you enter the correct formula, it gives you the answer to what you want. Instead of cracking your brain to find the average of some numbers, Excel does it for you and makes the job easy. I will use sample data to teach you on how to find the average of some numbers.

2	200	220	356
3	45	65	89
4	54	76	83
5			
6			

Sample data for finding of average value

To find the average of the above values is simple. The first step is to select the cell where you want to have your average value placed. Type the function =AVERAGE(and highlight the values you want to find average number from, introduce a close parenthesis) and then hit the Enter key of your computer keyboard. On doing that, the average value is inserted in the cell. Below is the function you are to type before pressing the Enter key in picture.

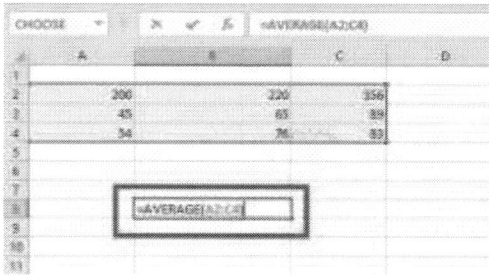

Average function in respect to the sample data

From the above photo, you can see the formula section indicated inside rectangle. When you hit the Enter button, you will see the average value inserted in that cell. If you are following up practically, the average value you will get is 132.

Also, you can find average value of some set of numbers by simply inserting the values or the cells' identity. Referencing to the main data sample, you can type =(A2+A3+A4+B2+B3+B4+C2+C3+C4)/9 in a cell where you want to have the average value inserted and then press the Enter key of your computer keyboard. On doing this, you will also get the average value of 132 inserted in the cell.

Exercise on Finding Average Value

From the experience you gained from my teaching on finding average of numbers listed in cells, find the average of the above numbers using the correct average formula.

Multiplication in Excel

Another calculation you can carryout in Excel spreadsheet is multiplication. This is simple just like other basic calculations I have discussed here. The multiplication sign recognized by Excel program is * and not alphabetical letter x. You need to know this for effective multiplication to be carried out in your spreadsheet.

To multiply two or more numbers, first select the cell you want the answer from the multiplication to be inserted. The next step is to multiply the cells that contains the values you are multiplying. I think it is better I use sample to pass this information. So, look at the screenshot of my spreadsheet with values to be multiplied.

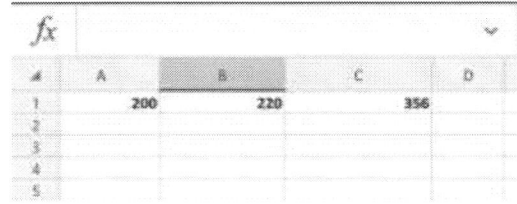

Data for multiplication

If you are to multiply the above values, first select a cell where you want the answer to the multiplication inserted. Then type the formula =A1*B1*C1 and then press the Enter key of your computer keyboard. On doing this, you will get the value for the multiplication.

You can also multiply the values directly. In that regard, just type =200*220*356 and then press the Enter key of your computer keyboard. You will see the answer to the multiplication right in front of you.

Understanding Division in Spreadsheet

There are many calculations that Excel users carryout and one of them is division. In this subheading, I will walk you through on how to divide values. Before I forget, the division sign Excel program understands easily is /. So, use that sign to make your divisions and get your answers.

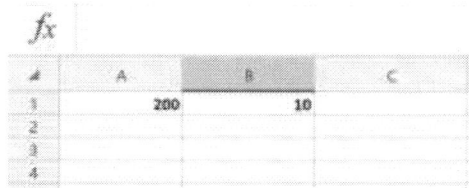

Data sample for division

Going with the above sample, I can easily divide a number with the other. If you are asked to divide 200 with 10. It is something simple to do. Just select the cell where you want to have the answer placed. The next step is to type the following formula in the cell:

=200/10

And lastly, press the Enter key of your computer keyboard. Immediately you do that, the answer to the division is inserted in the cell.

Another way you can divide in Excel is by quoting the cells instead of the values contained in the cells. From the above sample, you can just type =A1/B1 and then hit the Enter key of your computer keyboard. This action will still give you the same answer.

Finding Minimum Value

One of the things you can actually do with Excel formula is finding minimum value among many other numbers you have in different cells of the spreadsheet you are working on. Microsoft Excel makes that easy and simple. With prepared data, I will teach you on how you can get that done.

To find a minimum value from the numbers you have on Excel spreadsheet, select the cell you want the answer on the minimum value inserted. Below is the data sample I will be using to teach you on this area of interest.

Data from which we will find minimum value

After selecting the cell you want to have minimum value inserted, type =MIN(and then select the spreadsheet cells from which you want to find minimum value.

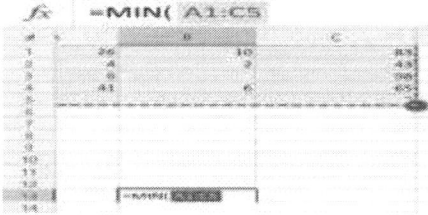

Selected cells from which minimum value will be found with part of minimum value formula

The next step is to close the minimum value formula with close parenthesis), and press the Enter button of your PC. Once you do this, the minimum value is inserted in the cell. Going with the data I have in the spreadsheet, the minimum value I got is "2" which is correct.

Exercise on Finding Minimum Value

Using the data in the spreadsheet below, find the minimum value applying the approach I taught you.

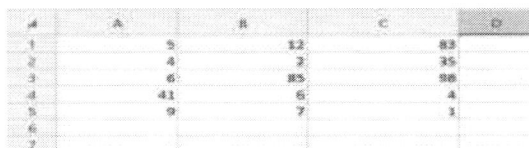

Data for your exercise

How to Find a Maximum Value

Just like the way I thought you on how to find a minimum value from series of numbers, you can still find a maximum value. All you need is to insert the correct function in a cell, select the series of numbers you want to find maximum value from, introduce your close parenthesis and lastly hit the Enter key of your PC keyboard. On doing that, you get the accurate result for that calculation.

Let me break it down the more with the sample I have below.

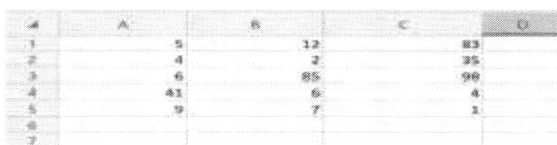

Sample data for finding maximum value

If I want you to find the maximum value from the above numbers in different cells of your spreadsheet, the first thing you are to do is to select the cell where you are to type the formula that will give you the answer you need at the end.

Type =MAX(and highlight all the cells containing values and once, introduce close parenthesis) to make the formula complete.

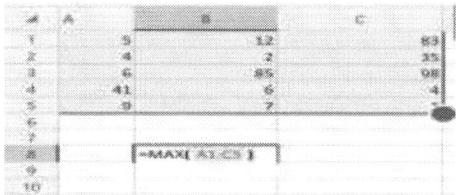

Complete formula for finding maximum value and the highlighted data

And lastly, press the Enter button of your computer keyboard. On taking this last step, the maximum number will appear automatically in the cell. This method is not that different from the others I have explained, so you can do it. If you are following up practically, the answer you will get on completing the above task is value 98.

Using Count Formula in Excel

Count formula is a formula that you can insert in a spreadsheet cell to give you the number of cells in your spreadsheet that have number values. It does not count alphabets but number values.

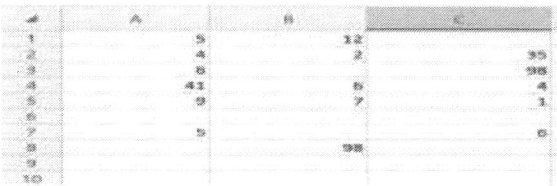

Data to be used for count explanation

From the above data, if you want to instruct your Excel spreadsheet to count the number of cells with numbers in them, first select the cell where you want the answer to your command to be inserted.

Type =COUNT(and select all the set of cells. The next step is to introduce close parenthesis) and then press Enter key.

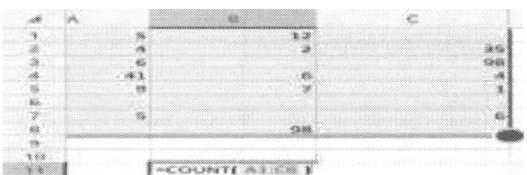

The highlighted cells and count formula

Excel software will count the number of your highlighted cells with number values in them and give you the answer immediately. If you are following up practically, the answer you will get is 16.

Exercise on Count

Having learned some things on count formula, using the data below, apply Excel count function to get an answer on the number of cells with numbers.

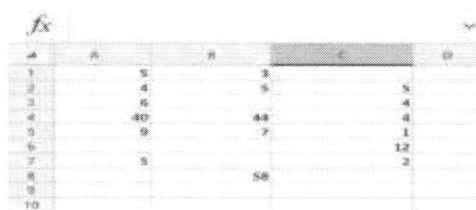

Data for count exercise

Understanding COUNTA Function

If you can remember, in the previous subheading, I stated that the Count function only counts all the cells with number values in them and give you the answer. Counta function counts both cells with numbers and alphabets in them. That is to say that it counts cells that have contents, be them numbers or letters.

I will use sample data to explain COUNTA function deeper.

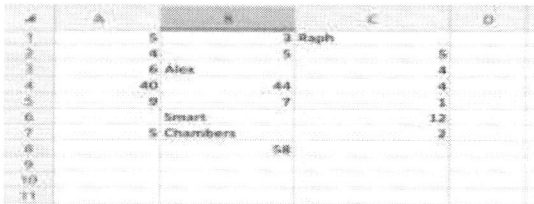

Data for COUNTA function

With the information above, if ask you to use COUNTA function to find the number of cells with content, it is something simple to do.

To start, select the cell where you want to have the answer to your command. Then, type =COUNTA(and select the cells of the spreadsheet. Introduce close parenthesis) to form a complete function just as seen in the spreadsheet below.

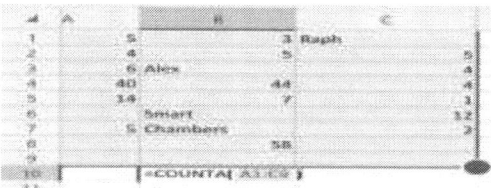

Highlighted spreadsheet cells with complete COUNTA function

The next and final step you are to take is to press the Enter key of your computer keyboard. On doing this, the answer indicating the number of highlighted cells with content will appear right there before you. With this, I believe you can perform as many COUNTA tasks as you want.

CONCATENATE Function in Excel

CONCATENATE function is an important function made available by Microsoft Excel developers. You may not be familiar with the word CONCATENATE but I will explain to you. CONCATENATE function in Excel allows you join two or three words as one unit.

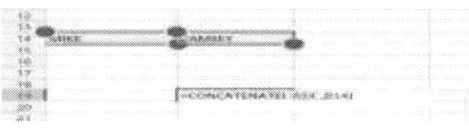

Data to explain CONCATENATE teaching

To use the CONCATENATE, first select the cell where you want to have the words appear as one at the end.

The next step you are to take after selecting the cell is type =CONCATENATE(and highlight the cells containing the words and separate the two words with comma, and then introduce close parenthesis) just as you can see in the screenshot below.

Progress in using CONCATENATE function

And lastly, press the Enter key of your PC keyboard. On taking this last step, the two words are joined as one. Making reference to the data I started this subheading with, below is the result in a spreadsheet cell.

The result achieved after using CONCATENATE function to join two names

Exercise on CONCATENATE

With the data below, use the CONCATENATE function to join the two names to become one unit.

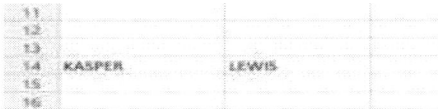

Data for the CONCATENATE task

"If" Function Explained

When I was a beginner in the use of Excel formula, I found it difficult to understand If function in detail. As of then, once I got to the "If" function section, I usually shied away. But as of today, it is a history. I use it and I like it.

You may ask, what is IF function? IF function is that function in Excel that allows you to make logical comparison between something and what you expect as the outcome. Take for instance a have a word "MANGO" in cell B1 of my Excel spreadsheet, I can use IF function to instruct Excel to say "Good" if the "MANGO" is in cell B1 and say "False" if the word "MANGO" is not in that cell.

Let me take it practically using the data I prepared in the spreadsheet below.

Data for IF function teaching

From the data above, I have the word "MONGO" in cell E2. So, using IF function, I will ask my Excel if really that cell E2 is containing the word MANGO it should give me return as "Good" otherwise let it say "False". This is what I have in a spreadsheet cell as shown in the photo below.

IF function with respect to the data I initially uploaded

Taking a look at the above information, the IF function I typed is =IF(E2="MANGO","Good","False"). On pressing the Enter key of my computer keyboard, the answer I got is Good. This is because the content "MONGO" is truly found in cell E2. If that is not found there, you will get "False" as the answer. Just feel free to practice with any content on IF function.

Finding Current Date and Time in Excel

Another important area in Excel which is part of formulas and function is current time. With Excel, you can find the current time without looking and the time app installed on your computer by default. This is a great development by Microsoft. All you need is to type few commands in the form of function and you will see the time inserted in a selected cell of your spreadsheet.

Take for instance you are working under an organization and your employer asks you to compose some information in Excel spreadsheet putting the time you finished with the work, Excel can help you do that. This is why I call it an intelligent software.

To insert the current real date and time in an Excel spreadsheet, these are the steps you need to take:

- First, select the cell where you actually want the current time inserted
- Type the function =NOW() and press the Enter button of your PC keyboard. This action will give you the exact date and time at that moment.

Chapter 6. Excel Functions

Excel Functions – Date and Time

- **Excel DATE Function**

You can use Excel's DATE function when you wish to acquire a date value using year, month, and day values as input arguments. It returns the serial number in Excel that corresponds to a given date.

- **Excel DATEVALUE Function**

The DATEVALUE function in Excel is best used when a date is recorded as text. The date is converted in text format to the serial number that Excel understands as just a date using this function.

- **Excel NETWORKDAYS Function**

The NETWORKDAYS function in Excel can be used to calculate the number of working days among two dates. Between the stated dates, weekends are not counted (by default, the weekend is Saturday and Sunday). It can also be used to omit specific holidays.

- **Excel NETWORKDAYS.INTL Function**

When you want to find the number of workdays among two dates, utilize the NETWORKDAYS.INTL function. Weekends and holidays, which the user can also set, are not included. It also gives you the option of specifying the weekends (You can, for example, designate Friday and Saturday as weekends, or merely Sunday as a weekend.)

- **Excel WEEKDAY Function**

In Excel, the WEEKDAY function is used to find the weekday for given date as a number. So, for instance, it will give you a number between 1 and 7 that corresponds to the weekday.

- **Excel WORKDAY Function**

When you want to have the date after a certain number of working days, you can use Excel's WORKDAY function. By default, the weekend is defined as Saturday and Sunday.

- **Excel WORKDAY.INTL Function**

When you need the date after a certain number of working days, use the "Excel WORKDAY.INTL" function. For example, you can use this method to make the weekend days apart from Saturday and Sunday.

- **Excel DATEDIF Function**

When calculating the number of days, months, or years between two dates, the DATEDIF function in Excel can be used. Calculating one's age is a nice illustration of this.

Excel Functions – Logical

- **Excel AND Function**

Whenever you want to evaluate multiple conditions in Excel, you can use the AND function. It only returns TRUE if all of the supplied conditions are met.

- **Excel FALSE Function**

FALSE is the logical value returned by the Excel FALSE function. It does not accept any arguments as input.

- **Excel IF Function**

The Excel IF Function is generally used when examining a condition and returning a value if this is TRUE and a different value, whether it is FALSE.

- **Excel IFS Function**

The Excel IFS Function may best be used when you wish to test numerous conditions at once to produce a response based on the results. This is advantageous since it eliminates the need for large, nested IF formulae that can be confusing.

- **Excel IFERROR Function**

The IFERROR function in Excel is best for formulas that result in an error. If the formula produces an error, you can select a value to display.

- **Excel NOT Function**

When you wish to reverse a value of the logical argument (TRUE/FALSE), you can use the NOT function in Excel.

- **Excel OR Function**

Whenever you want to evaluate multiple conditions in Excel, you can use the OR function. If some of the given conditions are true, it returns TRUE.

- **Excel TRUE Function**

The TRUE function in Excel delivers TRUE as a logical value. It does not accept any arguments as input.

Excel Functions – Lookup and Reference

- **Excel COLUMN Function**

When you need to find the column number with a certain cell in Excel, use the COLUMN function.

- **Excel COLUMNS Function**

The COLUMNS function in Excel can determine the number with columns in a range or array. It gives you a number that measures the total columns in the range or array you specified.

- **Excel HLOOKUP Function**

The HLOOKUP function in Excel is best used when you're seeking a similar data point in such a row, and once you've found it, you want to go down the column and get a value from the cell that's several rows just below the top row.

- **Excel INDEX Function**

When you assume the role (column number and row number) or even a value in some table, you can use the INDEX function in Excel to retrieve that value. This is indeed a powerful alternative to a VLOOKUP function that is frequently used with the MATCH function.

- **Excel INDIRECT Function**

When you have text references and wish to get the values through them, you can use the INDIRECT function in Excel. It returns the text string's provided reference.

- **Excel MATCH Function**

You can use the MATCH function in Excel to get the position relative or even a lookup value in such a list or an array. It produces a number indicating the lookup value's location in the array.

- **Excel OFFSET Function**

When you wish to retrieve a reference that offsets a particular number of columns and rows from the beginning point, you can use the OFFSET function in Excel. It returns a reference pointed to by the OFFSET function.

- **Excel ROW Function**

When you need to know the row number of the cell reference, use the Excel ROW Function. FOR INSTANCE, =ROW(B4) would be coming back four because it is in the fourth row.

- **Excel ROWS Function**

You can use the ROWS function in Excel when you need to know how many rows are in a range or array. The total rows in the supplied range or array are returned as a number.

- **Excel VLOOKUP Function**

The VLOOKUP function in Excel is best used when you're seeking a similar data point in some kind of a column, and once you've found it, you want to go to the right within this row and get a value from just a cell that's a specified feature vector to the right.

- **Excel XLOOKUP Function**

The Excel XLOOKUP function is an upgraded version of the VLOOKUP/HLOOKUP feature for Office 365 customers. It's used to look up and get data from a dataset, and it can take the place of most earlier lookup formulas.

- **Excel FILTER Function**

For Office 365 customers, the FILTER function is a new tool that allows you to swiftly filter and extract data depending on a condition (or multiple conditions).

Excel Functions – Text Functions

- **Excel CONCATENATE Function**

When you actually want to connect two or more characters or strings in Excel, use the CONCATENATE function. It can join text, cell references, numbers, or any combination of these.

- **Excel FIND Function**

When you wish to determine the position of a text string within another text string, you can use the Excel FIND function. It gives you a number representing the beginning of the string you're looking for in another string.

- **Excel LEFT Function**

To actually extract text from the left of a string, use the LEFT function in Excel. It returns the number of characters requested from the string's left side.

- **Excel LEN Function**

When you need to know how many characters are in a string, use the LEN function in Excel. When you need to know how long a string in a cell is, this is useful.

- **Excel LOWER Function**

When you wish to convert all uppercase letters in a text string to lowercase, use the LOWER function in Excel. The LOWER function does not affect numbers, special characters, or punctuation.

- **Excel MID Function**

To extract a particular amount of characters from the string, use the Excel MID function. It extracts a sub-string from the string and returns it.

- **Excel PROPER Function**

When you wish to uppercase the initial character of each word in Excel, use the PROPER function. The PROPER function does not affect numbers, special characters, or punctuation.

- **Excel REPLACE Function**

When you wish to replace a section of a text string with another string, you can use the REPLACE function in Excel. It returns the text string with the provided string replacing a portion of the text.

- **Excel REPT Function**

When you wish to repeat a sentence a specific number of times, you can use the REPT function in Excel.

- **Excel RIGHT Function**

The RIGHT function extracts text from the right side of a string. It returns the number of characters requested from the string's right side.

- **Excel SEARCH Function**

When you wish to find the position of a text string within another text string, you can use Excel's SEARCH function. It gives you a number symbolizing the beginning of the string you're looking for in another string. Again, there is actually no distinction between upper and lower case.

- **Excel SUBSTITUTE Function**

You can use Excel's SUBSTITUTE function to replace text in a string with the fresh specified text. It returns a text string in which the old text has been replaced with the new.

- **Excel TEXT Function**

Whenever you want to convert any number to text and display it specifically, you can use the TEXT function in Excel.

- **Excel TRIM Function**

You actually can use the TRIM function to eliminate leading, trailing, or double spaces in Excel.

- **Excel UPPER Function**

When you wish to change all lowercase letters in a text string to uppercase, use Excel's UPPER function. The UPPER function does not affect numbers, special characters, or punctuation.

Excel Functions – Math

- **Excel INT Function**

When you need a value rounded to a specific number of digits, users can use the ROUND function in Excel.

- **Excel MOD Function**

When one integer is actually divided by another, the MOD function in Excel can determine the residual. When one number is actually divided by another, it returns a numerical value that represents the residual.

- **Excel RAND Function**

You can use the RAND function in Excel to produce equally dispersed random integers between 0 and 1. It actually gives you a number between 0 and 1 as a result.

- **Excel RANDBETWEEN Function**

When you wish to produce uniformly dispersed random integers between a top and bottom range defined by the user, you can use the RANDBETWEEN function in Excel. It returns a number between the user-specified top and bottom ranges.

- **Excel ROUND Function**

When you need a value rounded to a specific number of digits, users can use the ROUND function in Excel.

- **Excel SUM Function**

To add all integers in a range of cells, use the SUM function in Excel.

- **Excel SUMIF Function**

When you wish to add the values in a range if a condition is met, you can use the SUMIF function in Excel.

- **Excel SUMIFS Function**

When you wish to add the values in a range if multiple stated conditions are matched, you can use the SUMIFS function in Excel.

- **Excel SUMPRODUCT Function**

When you wish to multiply two or more sets to arrays and then retrieve their sum, you can use Excel's SUMPRODUCT function.

Chapter 7. Excel Charts

We need Excel to store info for small & large businesses as well as personal data. Even though spreadsheets seem to be necessary for data processing, these are cumbersome and do not provide a clear view of data trends & relationships for team members. MS-Excel can assist them in converting spreadsheet details into graphs to create an intuitive research report as well as make rational business decisions.

MS-Excel 2022 helps you to build graphs & charts for almost any purpose. If you've created an MS Excel chart or graph, you could use the Template button to modify and adapt it to your specifications. Learn how to design a map in Excel 2022.

Here are the distinct forms & types of charts?

An Excel graph is a graphical representation of details in bars & several other shapes. It's a visual representation of data from such a workbook which could help you understand the data better than just gazing at the figures. A chart seems to be a powerful tool for visualizing data in a variety of formats, including Bar, Pie, Column, Doughnut shape, Graph, Zone sort, Radar graphs, Scatter dots, & Floor graphs. Using Excel to design a chart is a fast and effective method.

The Pie Charts

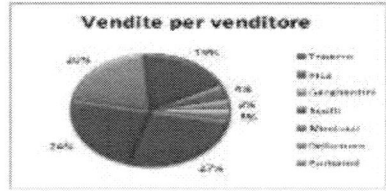

In certain cases, pie charts have been used to show the individual significance of different values while still adding the total value. A single collection of data is often used in a Pie chart.

To build a pie chart on some kind of data set using the 2022 versions of Excel, simply follow the instructions.

Pick the data set first from the A1:D2 range.

Over the Design tab of the Chart's type, pick the Pie logo.

Click Pie from the menu.

As a consequence, you will note the following.

Press on the pie so as to choose the whole pie. To take a section of the map away from the midline, tap on it.

Note: If you're designing a pie chart with a numeric mark, make sure cell A1 is blank first. While doing so, Excel will not treat the figures within column Too as a dataset &, therefore, will build the correct table automatically. If you like, you can add the content Year during step 1 after you've made the Chart.

Pick the A1:D1 category, then hold CTRL and click the A3:D3 category.

Press Delete on the icon at the bottom of the screen (following the preceding step of adding the graph).

Pick a good pie chart.

Pick a Data labeled check box by clicking the + icon on the desired section of the Chart.

On the appropriate side of the Chart, hit the paintbrush icon to change the color theme of the pie chart.

Right-click, that bar graph, then select Data Label Type from the context menu.

Uncheck value, verify Percentage, then press Middle to evaluate Name of Type.

Column Graphs

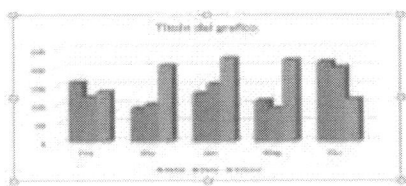

To design a column chart within Excel, you'll take the following steps:

Highlight the information you wish to use in the column chart. We picked the range A1:C7 for this case.

There in the toolbar at just the top of each page, select the Insert button. Click a chart from its drop-down menu by pressing the Excel Column chart option within Charts Category. For this case, we went with the very first column chart there in the 2-D Column section (regarded as Clustered Column).

All sales and expense statistics will be reflected in the column chart in the rectangle bar spreadsheet. Vertical blue lines represent sales values, while vertical orange lines represent costs. For certain vertical lines, their values of axes could be seen along the left side of the graph.

Last but not least, let's alter the column chart's explanation.

Click the "Chart Title" link towards the top of a graphic item to adjust the title. One ought to be able to notice that the title can be changed. Put the text you want to appear as the title here. Throughout this example, we will use the term "Sales & Expenses" to build a column chart.

The Line Charts

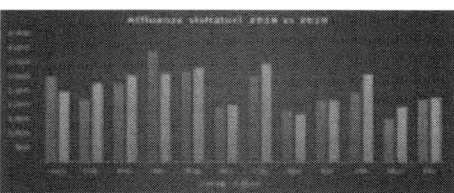

A bar chart, or a chart containing long bars, is a form of Chart used to visualize the significance of data over time. For example, the accounting team might chart a change in the quantity of cash the company has on hand over time.

First and foremost, ensure that the data is properly formatted before designing a bar chart.

Making use of Smart Draw Add column, pick line graph from the Graph menu.

Select the information file you have to use to generate the Chart, & Smart-Draw will create it for you instantly.

Utilizing Edit Graph tools & double-clicking an imported graph, one could easily alter the legend placement, description and modify the shape of a graph.

To design a bar graph through MS 2022, you'll take the following steps.

Highlight the information in the cell one would need to use to make a bar chart. We picked a range between A1 to C5 in this case.

Within the toolbar, just at the top of every page, click the Insert button. Select a chart through the drop-down menu by pressing the Excel Bar Chart icon in the Charts group.

For this case, we went with the very first bar chart there in the 2-D Column section (regarded as Clustered Bar).

You can also use the bar chart as in horizontal bar spreadsheet, which shows the retail as well as the shelf life of each product. Shelf life is represented by orange horizontal lines, while retail life is represented by blue horizontal lines. Through such horizontal lines, one could notice the axes' values at the bottom of the display.

Eventually, let's update the title of a bar graph.

Hit the "Chart Title" icon near the top of a graphic item to change the title. You ought to be able to recognize that the title can be changed. Put the text you want to appear as the title here. Throughout this example, we'll use the bar graph term as "Product Life."

The Area Charts

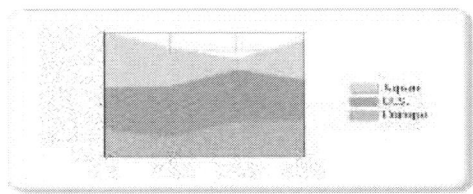

The same guidelines apply to Excel graphs & charts. Let's look at an example and see how to design an area chart.

For the area, we possess smart quarterly revenue results.

Choose the details

Go over to the Design category > then to Charts group > Select the Field graph.

Pick Clustered Area Graph through those in the region graph.

Scatter Charts

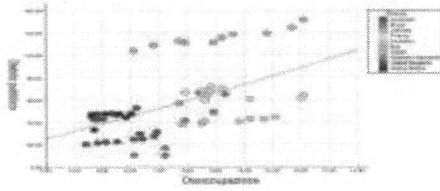

Choose a selection of worksheets from A1 to B11.

Upon this Insert page, hit the XY chart (Scatter) order logo.

Choose a graph subtype that would not include a graph.

The data within the XY table (Scatter) can be shown in Excel.

Double-check the Chart's data organization.

Check if MS has properly arranged the data by looking at the table.

On a Chart Tools Interface link, press the Turn Column/Row control key if you're unhappy with that of the graph's data entity- the data is backward or flip-flopped. (You can also experiment with the Turn Column/Row feature if you think it would be useful.) It's worth noting that the data is well organized. Increased advertising tends to be linked to increased sales, as seen in the graph.

Annotate the Chart as necessary. Make the Chart more attractive & readable by attaching those tiny blossoms to it. E.g., you might create a chart with a title or a description including the Chart's axes by using the Chart Title & Axes Titles controls. You can add a trend line by tapping the Add Chart Options menu upon a Trendline command icon. Pick the Interface click & then Add Chart Element option to display the menu of Add Chart Element. To access the Template page, one should first select an inserted map item or view a graph sheet.

The Trendline menu would appear in MS-Excel. By pressing on one of several of the accessible trendline options, one can specify the number of trendline and correlation estimates one may need. For e.g., to run any linear regression model, click the Linear button on the keyboard. A Trendline Graph Tools Configuration Tab in Excel 2k7 is where you introduce a trend line. To the scattering plot, add the regression equation.

To monitor how well trendline multiple regressions get measured, just use the ctrl key & text boxes within the Trendline Format panel. Place Intercept = checkbox or textboxes, e.g., may be used to force a trend line to intersect the x-axis after a certain point, such as zero. One could also have Forecast Forward & Primitive texts to emphasize that a trend line can be extended beyond and even before existing data.

Tap on the OK button.

You could barely see the regression details, so it all has been annotated, making it a lot clear.

Bubble Charts

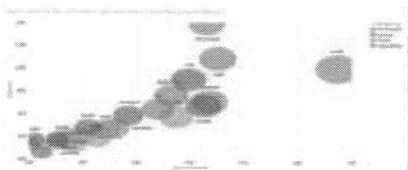

A Bubble graph appears similar to a Scatter graph, but with an additional third column to clarify the scale of the bubbles that depict data points therein data sequence.

The subtypes of the Bubble Chart are as follows:

- Bubbles
- A three-dimensional visual effect bubble
- Stock Chart

Stock style charts, as the name implies, will show price changes in stocks. Nonetheless, the Stocks Chart may be used to show changes in other figures, such as average rainfall or annual temperatures.

Place data into rows or columns in a specific order onto a worksheet to make a Stock graph. To make a simple low high stock chart, for e.g., arrange the data with such as Low-High- Close insert like as Column Names in such an order. The subtypes of the Stocks Chart are as follows:

- High-low-proximity
- Amount of high-low-close
- Volume of Open-High-Close
- Open- closer-Higher-Lower

Surface Charts

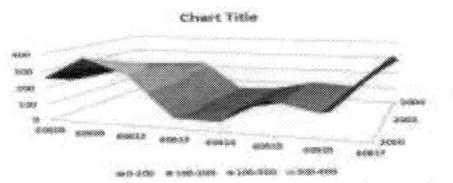

When you're trying to figure out which combinations of two variables are the best, a Surface graph will help. Colors & shapes depict regions in the very same way as they do in what seems like a topographic chart.

Follow these measures to build a Surface chart:

Ascertain that almost all divisions, including data series, correspond to integer values. On a worksheet, sort data along rows or columns. The following subtypes are represented on the surface chart:

- 3-D surface area
- Contours
- 3-Dimensional wireframe layer
- Wireframe's contour

Radar Charts

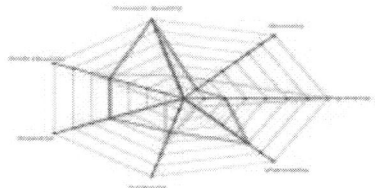

The Radar chart compares the values of several different data series. To generate a radar chart, arrange information in rows or columns upon a worksheet.

The below subtypes are included in the Radar chart:

- Radar & Markers
- Radar Loaded
- Simple Radar

Combo Charts

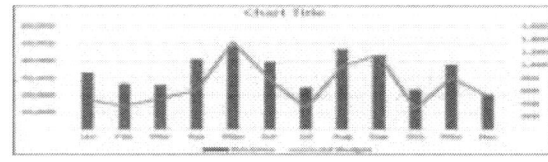

Such Combo graphs merge two or even more graph formats to generate data easier to understand, especially when there is a lot of it. It's visible from a secondary axis that's easier to read. To make a Combo table, put information in rows & columns upon a worksheet.

The variants of the Combo chart are as follows:

- Custom variations
- Panel Cluster – Line
- Secondary Axis Rows in a Grouped Panel
- Layered Field – Clustered Line

Excel Chart Customization

When the Chart Elements icon (with plus mark symbol) is selected in Excel 2k16-2k21, it presents a list including the main chart things that one can add to their Chart upon on the right-hand side of its built-in screen. To introduce an object to the table, hit the Chart Elements symbol to bring up a list of all Axis through Trendline in alphabetical order.

For e.g., to reconfigure the Chart's title, click on the Follow-up button on the Chart Elements toolbar associated to graph Title to display & choose between the below options upon its Follow-up menu:

Include or reconfigure the chart title just above the plot area, centered above the line.

Just use Focused Overlay Title to add or readjust the chart title at the top of a plot field.

More tools for opening the Format chart. To adjust almost every aspect of title formatting, use the choices that appear when selecting the Rows & Fill, Effects, also Scale & Assets buttons below. Title Choices & Script Layout & Fill, then Text Effects, also Dialog box tabs below Text Options there in the task pane.

The first column of this informational table includes the legend's keys.

How Significant Are the Charts?

MS-Excel has several automated tools, such as a graph function, to cope with all these other data storage values.

Anyone with accessibility to a spreadsheet could change data after it has been processed in the Excel database to view and express its significance. The chart function may be a key component of these systems.

Visualization

Spreadsheet managers may use Excel charts to create visual interpretations of data sets. Users can create various charts upon whom data is graphically depicted by highlighting a collection of data within the Excel spreadsheet & adding it to the graphing feature. Excel charts suitable for management/company presentations would help explain and convey the data set. A chart, rather than a table is containing lines of figures, which provide a clearer view about a set of data variables, allowing administrators to incorporate this interpretation into analysis or even plans.

Customization

MS-Excel simplifies the process of constructing charts from pre-existing data sets. Unless the spreadsheet has already changed data, the chart function might convert it to a graphic with just a minimum amount of user feedback. MS-Suggested Excel's Charts tool is an essential aspect of the phase. With only a few clicks, spreadsheet administrators can generate a chart, pick a chart type, and customize the names & axes.

Integration

When a business or other organization requires a database, data managed within MS Excel may be incorporated using the Excel chart function. For instance, whenever an Excel spreadsheet creates a chart using data in a worksheet, that Chart updates automatically as the data changes. This allows company managers & supervisors to keep track of their data as well as visualizations in a single feature, allowing them to quickly review reports.

Chapter 8.   Excel Pivot Table

There are two main components in creating Pivot tables:

- Defining fields or Field List
- Creating a table or Pivot Table Areas

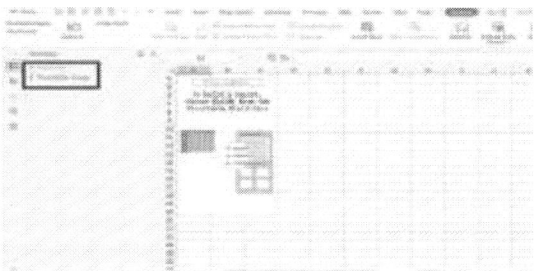

Understanding pivot tables and defining fields are important for two reasons.

1. It tells you what it is
2. It tells you how to get information into your Pivot table.

To understand this section, you need to know how Pivot tables work. The first reminder is that the Pivot table will be automatically sorted by the field that you are using, so if you choose a date field and then sort by another date field, the Pivot table will be automatically sorted by the date column.

The second thing to actually know is that you can define as many fields as you want for your Pivot table. This is what allows us to create a different Pivot table for each category of data, or topic.

Field List

The Pivot field list is the little icons that you see at the bottom of each column. You can tell which column is which by the little arrows on the left of the column. The Icon will change depending on what you want to do with it. You can add or delete data fields from this list by clicking the icon and dragging it up or down. If you click on the icon to highlight it, then a drop down box will appear where you can select what data that column should include in your table.

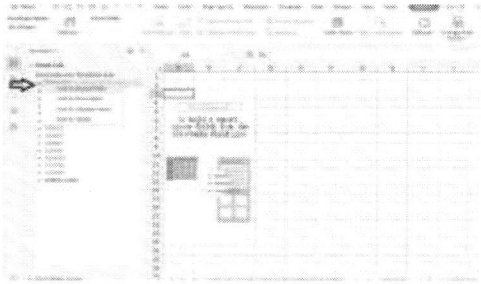

There are actually just a couple of ways to get to the Pivot field list.

1) From a Field list column, you can click on the little arrow beside the field name.
2) You can also drag a field from the main screen to the Pivot field list.

Pivot Table Area

The Pivot table is where all the data that was selected from the Pivot field list gets put together to make a table. The Pivot table has headings for each of the categories, and where each field for that category is placed in order under those headings.

There are four parts to a Pivot table, including the Filter area, Rows, Columns and the Values.

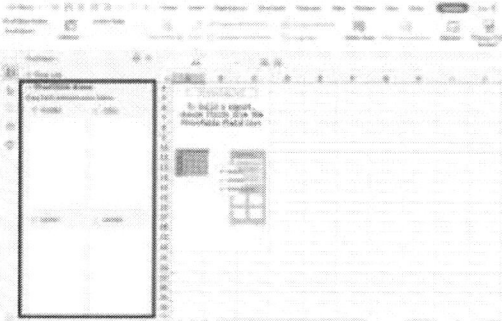

The Filter Area

The filter area appears on the right-hand side of the table and it is used to apply a condition to the data. For example, clicking the Product A filter in the first pivot table allows you to select a different Product range. The formula bar at the very top of Excel has a drop-down menu for automatically filtering data.

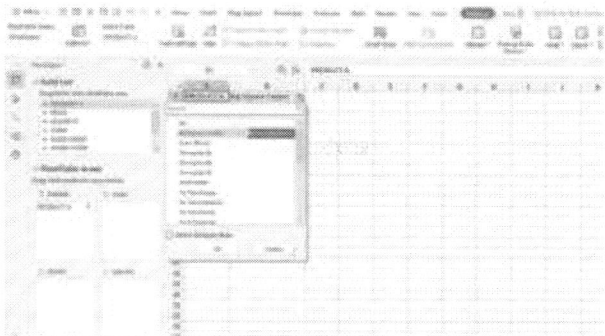

The Rows Area

The Rows area of an Excel spreadsheet shows the source data from which the Pivot table has been extracted. For example, the first column in the rows area shows the names of all the Sales Agent of the Product.

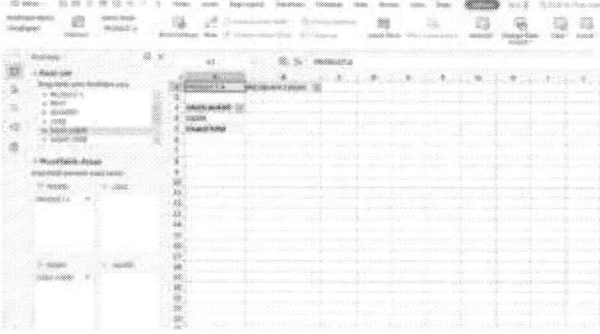

In above example, the name of "GEAN" appears under the row, it's because she's the sales agent of the said Product.

Now, let's filter the Product and select "ALL".

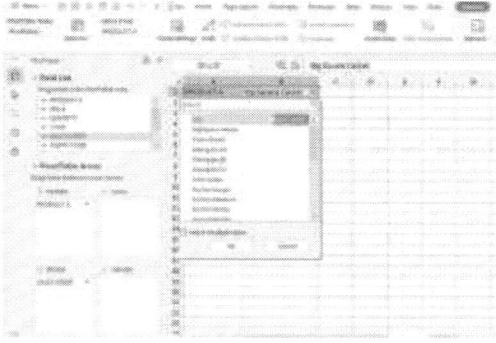

This is how it looks like:

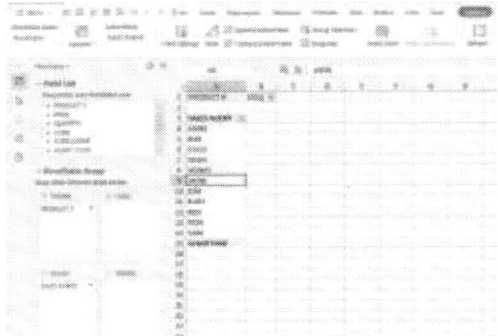

As you can see, all the name of the agents from the Product Range appears in our Pivot table. This is how to get information into your Pivot table.

The Columns Area

The columns of the Pivot table are arranged to show the information most meaningful to you. For example, in the second pivot table, the columns are arranged to show the Sales Code.

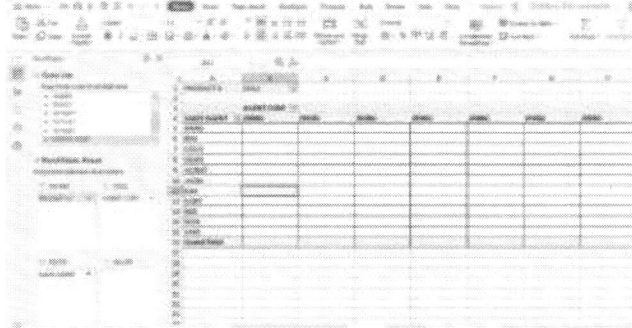

The Values Area

The Values Area is located at the bottom of a Pivot table and contains summary calculations created from the source data and can be used to further manipulate and analyze your worksheet data.

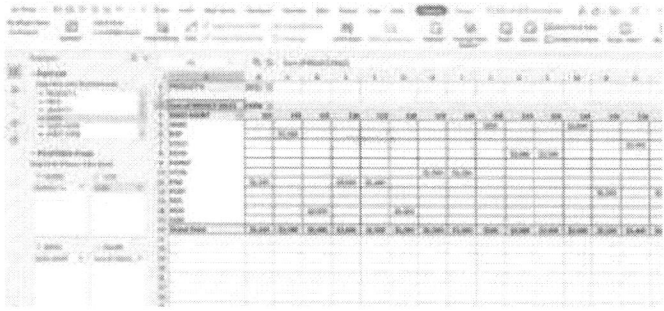

This is how your Pivot Table looks like.

Using the Commands to Accomplish a Pivot Table

Unlike with other spreadsheets, pivot tables are not limited to the dimensions of rows and columns. They can also have a value field that is split into multiple dimensions.

However, you will need to specify the settings for the value field and the value label to determine which cells in column A will be evaluated for values. To do this, open the design tab on top of your pivot table then click on value field settings symbol below fields.

You will then see the following settings:

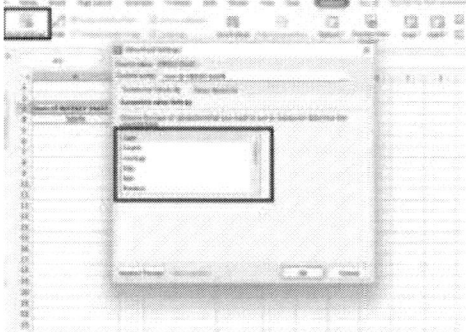

There are 11 different operations that you can choose from. Depending on your requirement, these are SUM, COUNT, AVERAGE, MAX, MIN, PRODUCT, COUNT NUMBERS, STDDEV, STDDEVP, VAR and VARP.

Sum: This operation will summarize the values in a field or column as a numerical value.

Count: This operation will count the number of values in a column or field and put it into another column.

Average: This operation will calculate the average of values from a specified row or column and place it in another cell.

Max: This operation will display the maximum value from a specified row or column and place it in another cell.

Min: This operation falls on the minimum value from a specified row or column and place it in another cell.

Product: Used to calculate the product of numbers that are found in different columns or rows, this option is selected if you want to multiply all the numbers that you have on your spreadsheet.

Count Numbers: This operation will count the number of numbers in a column or row and put into another column. This is functional if you want to display only a certain number of numbers both in your cell and on your pivot table.

STDev: is applied to calculate the standard deviation, which is a measure of how far the average value of a data set differs from the mean value.

STDVEP: This operation turns out when you have calculated the standard deviation, this will calculate the value of standard deviation and place it into another field.

VAR: This operation calculates the variance from numbers in different columns or rows, this calculation falls on the variance of the data.

VARP: This value returns the variance of numbers of the population. This is usually used in the context of being a function that is performed on a population.

What is the value field setting used for?

The main purpose of the value field setting is to extract the details that you need from all the values in a row or column. These includes:

- Summarizing data in a column or row as a whole
- Allowing you to filter out only one column or row in your pivot table
- Calculating the average and standard deviation of data in cells

The value field setting determines which operation to perform when extracting values with the extract function. There are different types of value field settings as discussed above, and we will look at all Values.

For example, you want to find how much does the Agent got on selling the product in a week. Usually, the whole table is analyzed to find out which product sold the most. Instead of searching for each one of the individual columns and rows, it's a lot easier to create a pivot table analyzing sales by each product.

To get started with it, here's what we do:

1. Make sure you have a clear data with Headings on each column and no empty rows or columns in the center of your data set and set your data is set as table.

2. Rename your table so you won't get confused.

3. Go on the data tab and click Pivot Table, A window will pop up. You'll be asked to choose a location where it will be saved and then hit OK.

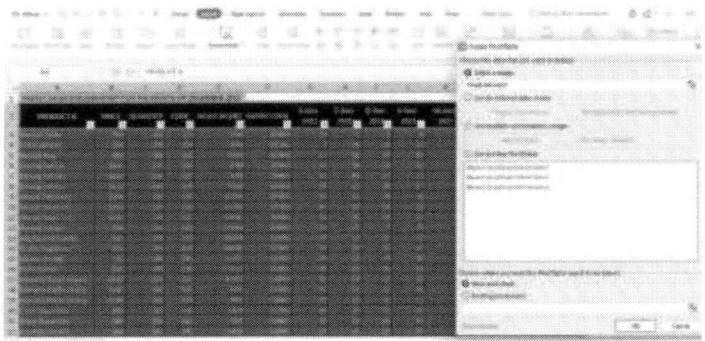

Excel will create your pivot table for you like this:

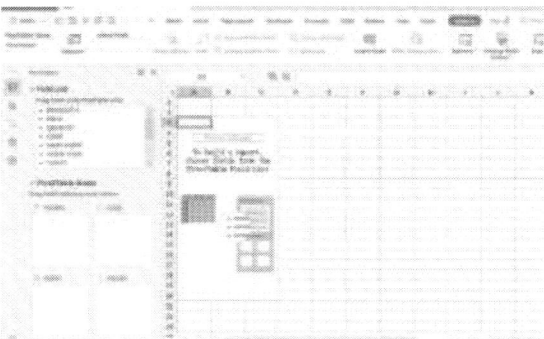

A blank pivot table appears on your worksheet. This is your work area where you will define all your fields and how they are broken down into individual items for analysis.

4. After you see your pivot table. Select any cell in the pivot table and click on Fields, you'll see a drop down list of options to organize your data set into columns.

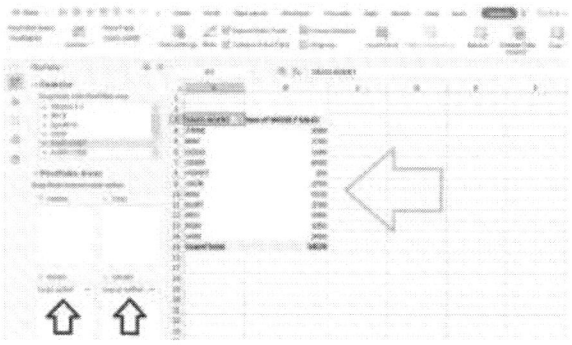

Sum Value

This operation will summarize the values in a field or column as a numerical value. For this example, we will set the Sales Agent in 'Row' field and Weekly Sales in 'Value' field. This is how the Sum Value Works.

Another sample using the Sum Value is to find out how many Products does the certain Agent sold for every day.

To apply this, you will need to set the data on each table. For this, let's place the Sales Agent on Filters and set the Dates in Value area.

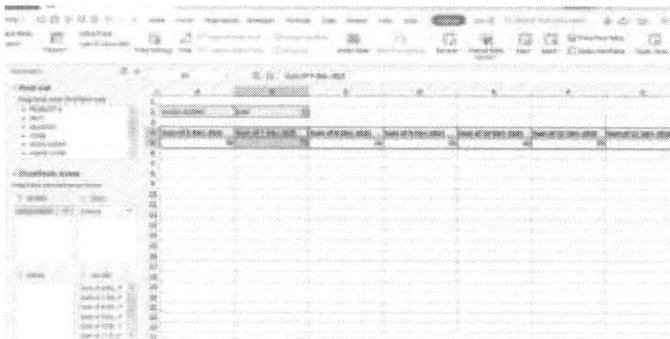

There you go, we got how many products that Agent Kim has sold every day.

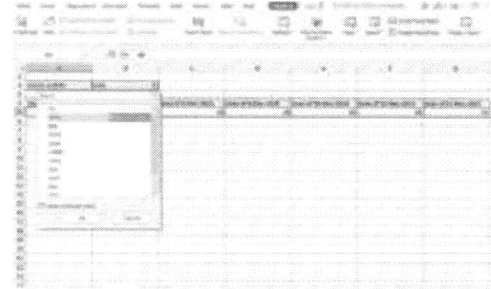

Let's check out the other agents by filtering the name. Let's choose ANNE with the products under her department.

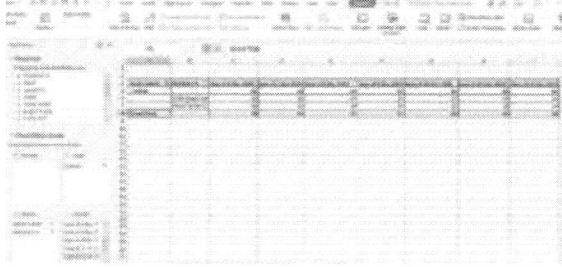

To check whether our table is correct, let's look in our data source. To do this, just double click the result value and you will be directed into a new spreadsheet showing the summarize data.

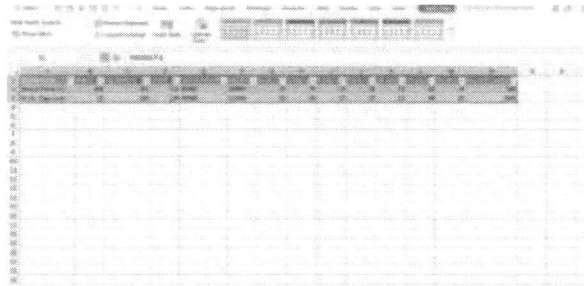

Count Value

The count operation will count the number of values in a column or field and put it into another column. For example, we have a row for sales agents, but we only want to see the total count of the products under their department.

To do this, in the Value Field Settings window, place the Product table and set the Field Settings in Count Value.

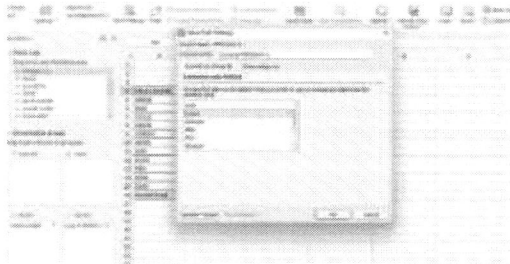

The table should look like this:

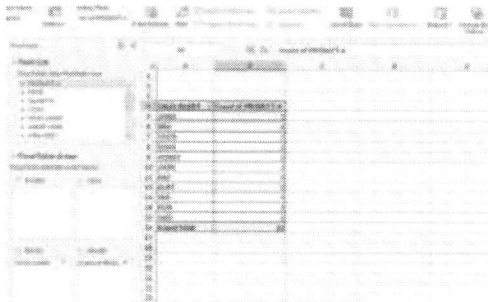

What if we would also like to know what kind of Products under their department? To do this, just simply add your Product data in Row.

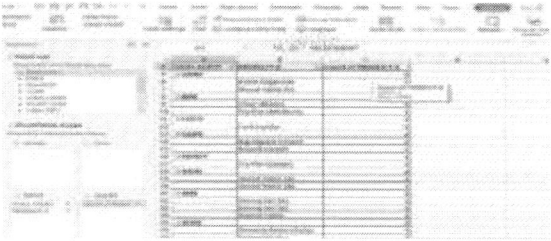

This explains that Agent Anne has two kinds of products under her department.

Average Value

This operation will calculate the average of values in a row or column and place it into another field. For example, the average price of each product under their department.

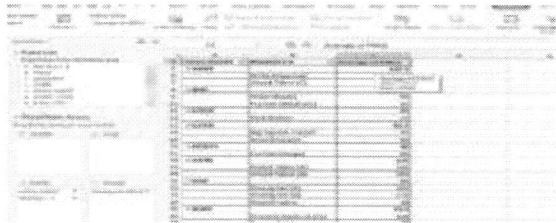

Max Value

This operation will display the maximum value from a specified row or column and place it in another cell. For example, you will have a sold data for every day. The sales for each day can be calculated and recorded, but instead of adding up the numbers, we only want to see which the maximum quantity is sold value per day. You can actually do this by simply clicking on 'Max' value under 'Value Field Settings'. Then you will see in your pivot table that the maximum of all the sales is placed in another cell.

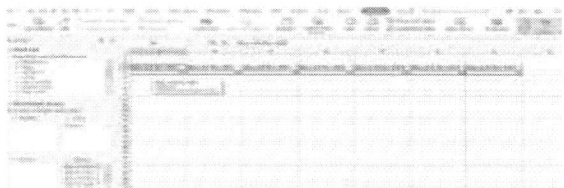

Min Value

This operation falls on the minimum value from a specified row or column and place it in another cell. For example, it is the same as Max, but this time instead of displaying the maximum value from a specified row or column and place it in another cell, we want to find out the minimum value from a specified row or column and place it in another cell. We simply click on Min value under 'Value Field Settings' then our obtained data will be placed into another cell.

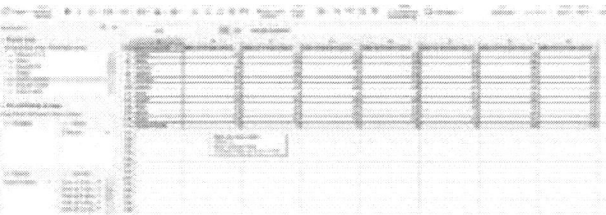

Product Value

This operation will calculate the product of numbers that are found in different columns or rows, this option is selected if you want to multiply all the numbers that you have on your spreadsheet.

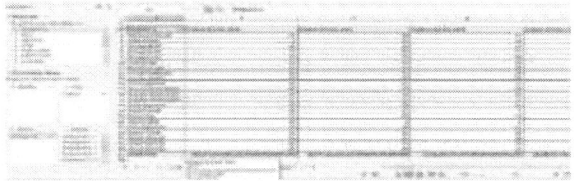

Count Numbers Value

This operation will count the number of numbers in a column or row and put into another column. For example, you have one column for the product and you have a list of all salespeople assigned to each product. You can calculate the total number of salespeople from this list and put it into another column.

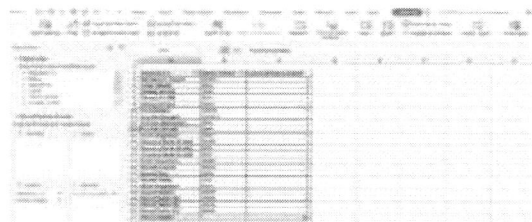

StdDev Value

StdDev is actually used to calculate the standard deviation, which is a measure of how far the average value of a data set differs from the mean value. In other words, it is used to test whether your numbers will be distributed normally.

For example, you have sales weekly and you want to find out the standard deviation. Firstly, calculate the average value of your weekly sales and another set of value of your weekly sales to calculate the standard deviation. Then you will see in your pivot table the result of standard deviation of your weekly sales

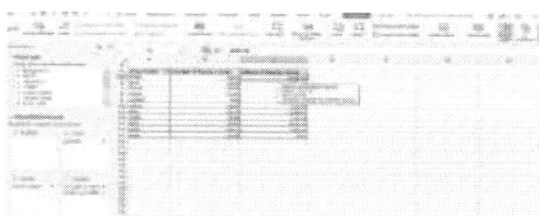

StdDevp

This operation turns out when you have calculated the standard deviation, this is an additional option that you can use to see the standard deviation on all or only some of your rows or columns.

Var Value

VAR: This operation calculates the variance from numbers in different columns or rows, this calculation falls on the variance of the data. For example, you to find out the variance of your weekly sales.

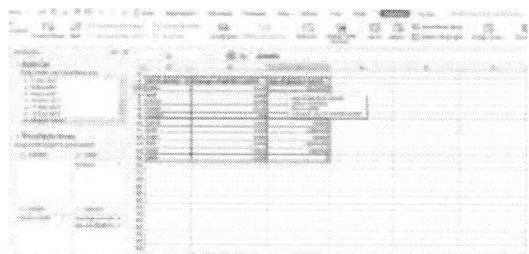

Varp Value

This value returns the variance of numbers of the population. This is usually used in the context of being a function that is performed on a population.

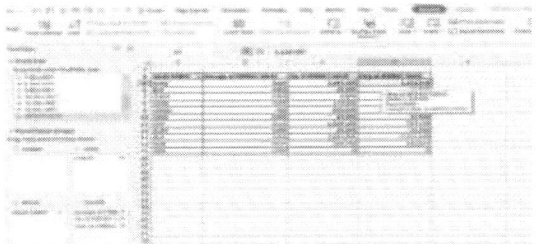

Excel Tips for Pivot Tables

Here are a few Excel tips for Pivot tables that can help you get the most out of your data.

1. Be honest with yourself. If you have incomplete information, do not include that data in your pivot table. This will prevent inaccurate calculations from being done and could lead to interpretation issues later.
2. Be careful about what you include in a Pivot table. The numbers Excel looks at will change as you change what variables are included in the table.
3. Don't forget about where your data is! If your data are in a different location, then be sure to tell Excel where to find it.
4. Use a consistent column heading to help keep your Pivot table efficient. If you can, use the same naming convention for each column so that it's easier to see the relationship between them. This can be obliging if you want to export your Pivot data.
5. Don't forget about summary functions and the different options you have for them. These are great ways to simplify your numbers and help you understand what direction your business is going in.

Chapter 9.   Getting More in Excel

In the past chapters, I walked you through on how to perform some basic tasks in Excel spreadsheet. All these I taught you in simple English. You were able to learn some basics including understanding on the default tabs made available by Microsoft in Excel, how to add and remove tabs, how to select cells content and the entire spreadsheet, editing and deleting content of a spreadsheet, how to export files initially saved in Excel format in PDF, cells extension and AutoFit, detailed understanding on Quick Analysis tool and sample, and few other areas.

In this chapter, the teaching continues. I will teach you on how to complete other tasks in Excel which at the end will make you a better user. As usual, I will take them step by step for your proper and easy comprehension.

How to Insert Rows and Columns

There may be a time you are typing list of names in a spreadsheet and make a mistake and jump one or two names. Instead of deleting some names you have previously typed to enter that name you missed in its rightful position, the best thing you can do is to add either row or column and lastly insert the information you missed.

In this subheading, I will walk you through on how you can insert row and column in a spreadsheet you are working on to complete a particular task of your choice.

Let us start with how to insert row in a spreadsheet. As a reminder, rows are numbered horizontally. To insert a row, select a row. When you select a particular row, the new one to be insert will be above it. Let me use the spreadsheet below to explain it for more practical understanding.

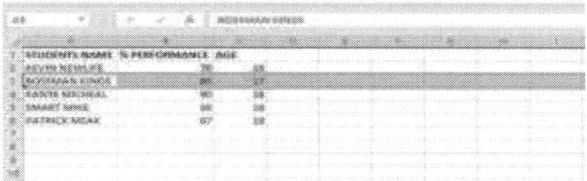

About to insert a row as row number 3 is selected

Know that to select a row, take your cursor to that number and click on it once. Referring to the above screenshot, the row number 3 is selected, and before I did that, I dragged my computer cursor/pointer to that number 3 and clicked on it.

As the row is selected, right-click on it. You will see some options including Cut, Copy, paste options Insert, Delete and others. Click the Insert command. Immediately you do that, a new row is inserted. Referring to the above screenshot, the new row that will be inserted is row number 3 while the selected automatically moved to become row number 4. This is shown in the photo below.

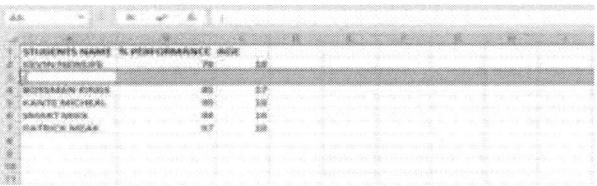

The newly inserted row 3 is still empty

At the insertion of the new row, you can then start entering the information you want to have in it. That is all on how to insert new row in an Excel spreadsheet. Use this approach to insert as many rows as you want in a spreadsheet you are working on.

Let me guide you on how to insert new column in a spreadsheet. It follows similar approach of inserting row in a spreadsheet.

Columns are labelled with alphabetical letters in vertical order. To insert a new column in a spreadsheet, select the column you want to insert the new column. To select the column, just click the letter that starts that column just as you can see that in the photo below.

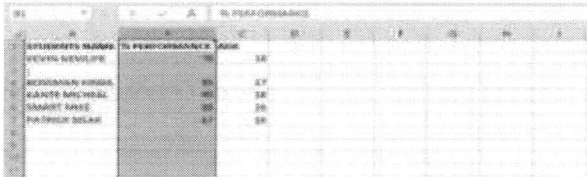

A selected column where a new column to be inserted will be positioned

Referring to the photo above, the place I am to right-click is the letter B. And from the options that are displayed after the right clicking, select Insert. As soon as you take this last step, new column is inserted just as you can see in the photo below.

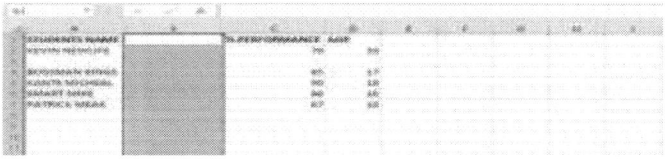

92

The spreadsheet with a newly inserted column B

Hiding Rows and Columns

One of the beautiful things about Microsoft Excel is that you can make changes without any stress. Even if you made any mistake while entering some data, you can easily get that mistake corrected by hiding the information. It is a good work by Microsoft team of software developers.

If you entered some data in a row of a spreadsheet and later want to make that row unnoticed, it is possible. Instead of deleting the information one by one, you can just hide the whole row. This makes the work easy for we users.

To hide any row in your spreadsheet, these are the steps you are to take:

Select the row you want to hide. Referring to the photo below, I want to hide row 2 and that is why got it selected. Know that you can select a row by just clicking the row number once. In the photo below, I selected row 2 by just clicking the number "2".

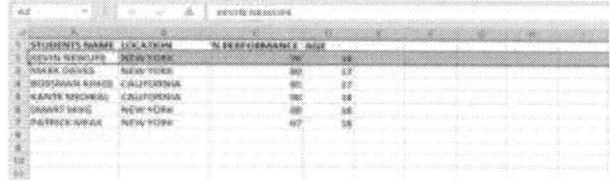

Selected row 2 ready to be hidden

As the row is selected, right-click on it and select Hide. As soon as you click Hide, the selected row becomes hidden.

To hide a column involves similar steps. The first step is to select the column you want to hide.

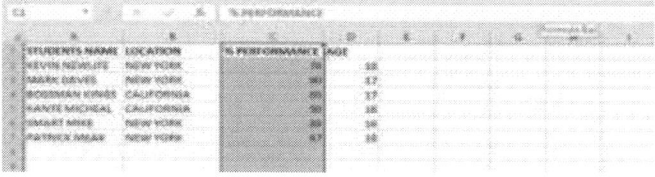

Selected column C to be hidden

Referring to the above photo, column C is selected. The next step to take is to right-click the selected column. You will see some options, just click Hide. Once you do that, the column will be hidden.

Unhiding Rows and Columns

I just walked you through on how you can hide row and column of your Excel spreadsheet. That was easy to follow guide. On the other hand, you can unhide those hidden rows and columns if you want to have the information the way it was before you did the hiding.

To unhide any row, take your computer cursor to the position of the hidden row and right-click on it. You will see some options, just select Unhide.

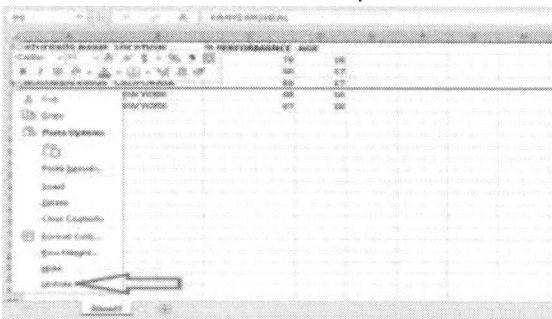

Select the Unhide command

Immediately you select the Unhide command, you will see the previously hidden row appear again.

On the other hand, you can unhide any column you have hidden before now. It is a simple task to complete. To unhide any hidden column, gently take the cursor of your computer to the line of the hidden column. Right-click that place and you will see some options. Click the Unhide command. As you do this, the previously hidden column will appear again in its previous position.

Working on Ribbons

There are some ribbons that are made available in Microsoft Excel spreadsheet. By default, ribbons are chosen to show all the tabs and commands in Excel. But for some reasons, some people choose different ribbon settings. Some choose to show only tabs while some choose the Auto-hide ribbon settings.

When I was newly using Excel as a beginner, I ran into problem by mistakenly choosing the Auto-hide Ribbon option. I found it difficult to change this to its normal state of showing both the tabs and commands. It was after making some research that I found a solution to the challenge. It really gave me a tough time because I began to think that my Excel desktop app developed technical issue.

So, let me go into details on how you can make changes to the ribbon of your Excel application.

How to Hide Excel Ribbon

To hide Excel spreadsheet ribbon, first click the Ribbon Display Options button

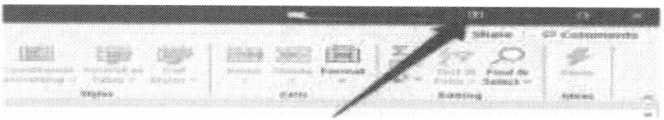

The Ribbon Display Options button pointed by an arrow

If your computer is running Windows 11 Operating System, the position of the Ribbon Display Options icon looks a little bit different. The icon is at the top extreme-right of the Excel interface. The position is indicated in the photo below:

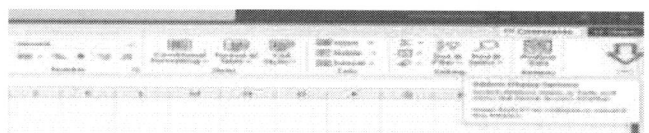

The position of Ribbon display Options button in Windows 11

On clicking the Ribbon Display Options, you will see some commands displayed. This is shown in the photo below.

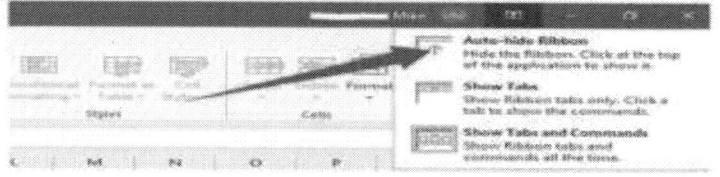

About to select a ribbon option

From the options, select Auto-hide Ribbon. When you select this option, all the major tabs and commands made available on your spreadsheet app by default will not be there again. The photo below is how the new interface will look.

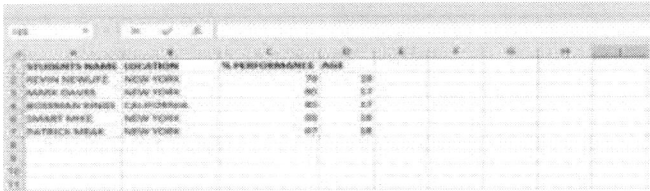

The new interface of Microsoft Excel software after Auto-hide Ribbon is chosen

From the above screenshot, you will see that the major tabs and commands made available by default have disappeared. This is because I chose the Auto-hide Ribbon option.

Guide on How to Display Only Tabs on Excel Spreadsheet

For the reason best known to some Excel users, many choose the option to display only the major tabs on the ribbon section of the interface instead of having both tabs and commands the way they are made available by default. According to some users, they say they prefer choosing the option to show only major tabs because it gives them enough space to work.

To display only tabs, click the Ribbon Display Options button which is at the top-right.

The Ribbon Display Options button pointed by arrow

On clicking the Ribbon Display Options button, you will see some options. Select Show Tabs. On selecting the Show Tabs, you will see only the tabs of the spreadsheet appear just as I have in the screenshot below.

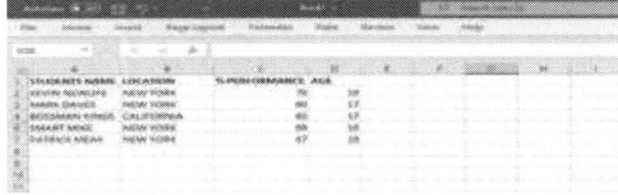

The interface of Excel spreadsheet on selecting Show Tabs

From the above photo, the tabs displayed are File, Home, Insert, Page Layout, Formulas, Data, Review, View and Help without including the commands under each of the tabs. This will take us to the next subheading.

How to Display Both Tabs and Commands on a Spreadsheet

As I stated before now, by default, your Excel spreadsheet is designed in a way that it shows but the tabs and commands that make it up. This allows you to actually use any of the buttons you want as quick as possible.

So, if for any reason you changed the way the ribbon is displayed and you want to take it back to its original state of showing both tabs and commands, it is very possible.

To do that, click the Ribbon Display Options button. This action will display three options for you. Select Show Tabs and Commands option. On doing this, your spreadsheet displays both commands and tabs. You will see the interface appear as below.

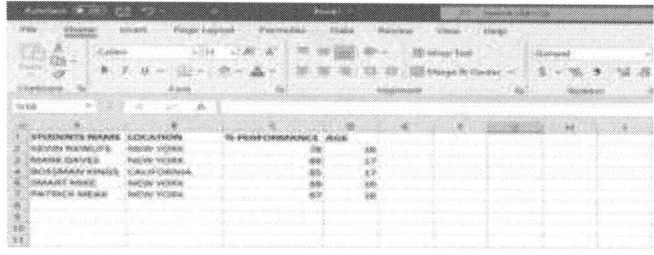

Both tabs and commands are displayed

Adding Comments in Cells

One of the beauties of Excel spreadsheet is that you can add comments in cells that contains data to explain what you have in that cell. Comments are added in cells to explain the data you have in that cell further. Sometimes, if you observe that the recipient of that Excel file may not understand the data you have in some spreadsheet cells, it is important you add comments to explain your points further.

Take for instance you have two workers in your company that bear same name but occupies different working positions. If for instance you are composing the names of your workers which involves these two workers with the same name, you can differentiate between the two using comments. Maybe in each of the comments, you add a note on the position occupied by each. This will make a difference. Once the recipient brings the cursor of the computer to the comment symbol of the cell, it will display what is contained in the comment.

To add a comment in a cell, take these steps:

Click the cell you want to add comment in. On selecting the cell, click Insert tab followed by Comment which is positioned at the top-right of the interface.

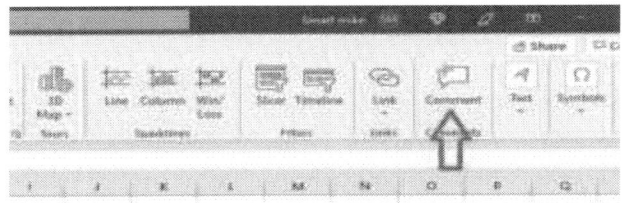

The comment command pointed by arrow

On clicking the Comment command, the comment space will appear at the cell. Start typing the note you want to add as comment.

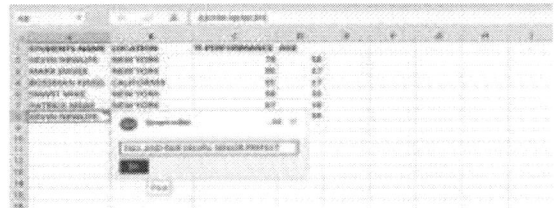

Added comment in a cell ready to be posted

When you are done with adding of your comment, click the Post icon which is an arrow that points towards the right. Adding comments in any cell clarify some things. Once you click the Post icon, click out and continue with other things you are doing.

How to View All Comments in a Spreadsheet

If someone sent mail to your email address containing spreadsheet file, how do you know that there are comments in that spreadsheet? On the other hand, how do you view the comments to know their contents?

First, to know if there are comments in that spreadsheet, you will see cell or cells with command symbol. This comment symbol is usually in purple color. The comment symbol is indicated in the photo below. You might have been seeing this symbol but did not know what it is.

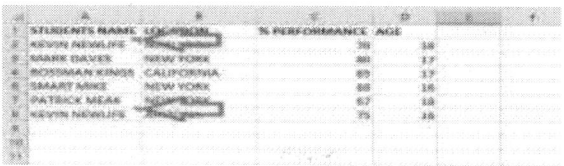

Comment symbol on cells pointed by arrows

To see the comment attached on each cell, place the pointer of your computer on it comment symbol, you will see the note attached to the cells.

Alternatively, you can see all the comments in a spreadsheet once. To do that, click the Home tab of your spreadsheet. The photo below shows the position of the Comments command.

The Comments command indicated

On clicking the Comments command, you will see all the comments in the spreadsheet appear by the right margin of the spreadsheet.

File Sharing in Excel

File sharing is important when it comes to using of some applications. Take for instance I own a company and every month, I share information on the performance of all my employees with other top officers properly prepared in Excel spreadsheet. The share button makes it easy to achieve this. In this section I will put you through on how you can share your prepared Excel document without stress.

To share your spreadsheet file after its composition, click the Share button at the top right.

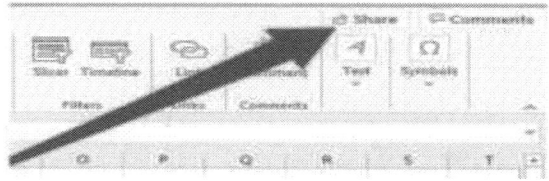

The Share button pointed by arrow

On clicking the Share button, Excel will request how you want to share the file. You are given the options to share the file on OneDrive, share as attach in workbook format or as PDF.

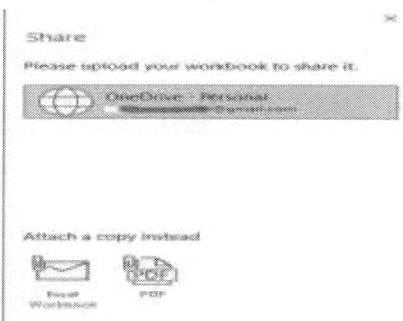

Options available to share Microsoft Excel file

Out of the 3 options, just select the way you want to share your file.

Sharing Your Excel File on OneDrive

As I stated earlier, one of the ways through which you can share the file you composed in Excel is via sharing it on OneDrive. For you to succeed in sharing your file on OneDrive, that file is uploaded in Microsoft cloud. When uploaded on cloud, you can access the file from any part of the world once you log into your OneDrive account.

To share your Excel file on OneDrive, click the share icon at the top right corner of your Excel spreadsheet.

The Share button pointed by arrow

On clicking the Share button, select the OneDrive option. If you are not signed into your OneDrive account automatically, you will be required to type your email address and password to sign in. Choose the folder you want to save the file and then save it there.

Sharing Excel File as Attach

If you can remember, on clicking the Share button at the top right of your Excel spreadsheet interface, you are given the option to share the file as attach. In that option to attach a copy, you are given the options to attach a copy in spreadsheet format and in PDF.

Let me assume you want to attach a copy in spreadsheet format, so click the Excel Workbook under the Attach a copy instead. Follow the prompt to be logged into your mail. Space will actually be provided for you to type the email addresses of the people you want to share the file with. Enter their email addresses. When you are done with that, click send button for the Excel file to be shared with them.

These are the steps you need to take to share Excel with your OneDrive account and with other recipients.

Adding Notes in Cells

Notes do the same job as comments. Both are ways to add additional information in any cell to explain further to your recipient or even yourself. So, whichever one you choose between notes and comments, they are all fine.

To add a note to any cell of your spreadsheet, first select the cell you want the note added. Know that selecting a cell is just by a click on that particular cell.

As the cell is selected, click the Review tab followed by Notes command.

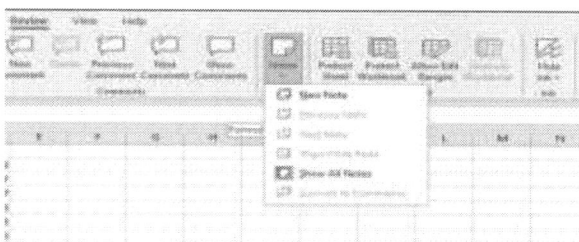

Notes command selected

On clicking the Notes command, you will see some options. Just click New Note. Type the note in the space provided.

When you are done typing your note, you can drag it to any part of your spreadsheet so that it does not distract you from reading other contents of your spreadsheet. On adding the note, you will notice a red color symbol in the cell. That is evidence that there is added note in that cell.

As an added information, on adding note on a cell of a spreadsheet, the note will appear on the spreadsheet. To hide that note so that it does not distract you from doing other things, click the Review tab followed by Notes command. Select the option Show/Hide Note. On doing that, the added note becomes hidden.

How to View Notes

What if someone sent an Excel file to you and on opening it wants to find out if there are notes that are added in the spreadsheet. How do you go about that?

To view all notes in a spreadsheet, click Review tab followed be Notes. As you click the Notes tab, select Show All Notes. On taking this last action, you will see all the notes in the spreadsheet appear at the spreadsheet clearly.

How to Delete a Note

If after adding a note to a cell, and you feel you do not need that note again, you can get it deleted. For you to delete a note, click on the cell that contains the note for it to be selected. The next step is to right-click on that cell. You will see some options displayed. Just select the option that reads Delete Note. On doing this, the note that was added in the cell is deleted.

Spreadsheet and Workbook Protection

Does your bank send your statement of account to your email address every month? If your bank does that, you will discover you don't just open that file without typing any security password to access it in some cases. It can be few digits from your account number.

Security is very important in most things we do in life. The reason you lock your doors properly before you sleep every night is because of security. The reason you use password, pattern or PIN to lock your smartphone is because of Security. Security is important for our safety.

In respect to that, Microsoft built their Excel with good security feature so that someone doesn't just view what is contained in the file without password. If you are sending the earnings of your workers to some top officers in your company, there may be need to lock it with password because that is sensitive information that everybody does not need to access. On sending the file to the top officers, you share the password with them which they need to insert before they can view the content. Any other person without the password cannot view the data contained in the file.

How to Lock a Worksheet with Password

Whether worksheet or spreadsheet, we are talking about the same area of interest. To protect a spreadsheet, just click the spreadsheet name example sheet1, sheet2, sheet3 (but if it's only one sheet in that workbook, no need to click the spreadsheet name).

The next step you actually need to take is to click the Review tab of Excel. Click Protect Sheet command. This action will open sheet protection dialog box which I have in the photo below.

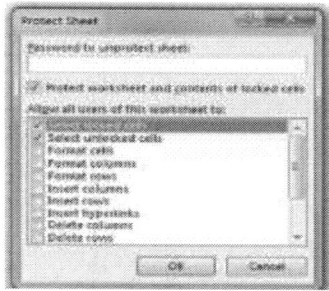

The sheet protection dialog box

In the space for Password to unprotect sheet, just type the password you want to use to lock the worksheet. Click Ok button. Excel will request you type the password you previously typed for the sheet protection. Just enter the same password and click OK button again. Once Excel confirms that the password you re-entered is correct, the sheet becomes locked. That is all on how you can protect a worksheet.

How to Secure Workbook with Password

The same way you locked a worksheet with password, you can still secure your workbook with password. Know that workbook has more than one spreadsheet inside of it. I explained this in chapter 1 under terminology used in Excel.

To protect a workbook with password, take these steps:

Click the Review tab of your Excel. As you click the tab, you will see some commands, just click the Protect Workbook command. This action will open a dialog box. In the space for you to type the password you want to use to lock the workbook, just type the password you can remember. Click the OK button at the bottom part of the dialog box. Excel will demand you repeat the password again. Type the same password and click OK button. On doing that, the entire workbook becomes protected with the password.

Understanding Smart Lookup Feature

Smart Lookup is a beautiful feature that Microsoft integrated into their new version of Excel software. As the name implies, this command allows you to lookup some words in a smart way. You do not need to start looking for the meaning or detailed understanding of some words in a separate dictionary. Smart Lookup command can do the job for you. But know that for smart lookup to work, your computer must be connected to internet.

To use Smart Lookup, click the Review tab of your spreadsheet. Click the Smart Lookup command. A space will actually be provided for you to type the word you want to search about. On typing the word, Smart Lookup brings up the meaning of the word in detail plus external resources to read more on the word in some cases. Feel free to use the tool when necessary.

Chapter 10. Excel Tips and Tricks

A spreadsheet is more than just a set of numbers on a tab. To make your own spreadsheets look professional, easy to understand, and visually pleasing to your audience is important.

Your Excel presentation will not impress your audience if it appears clumsy and boring, no matter how many hours of analysis went into it or how relevant the knowledge stored inside is.

The secrets hidden in this chapter can come in handy whether you are making a report for personal use, passing details to your team, or sharing with your project manager. Let us glance at some of the latest Excel presentation tips to help you make eye-catching spreadsheets.

1. **Search For Templates Online**

If you are actually a busy person and you would like to make the most out of your spreadsheet without losing time, you can choose from a variety of purpose-specific templates that include attractive styles, fonts, and colors. To work on a template, simply insert your values, and you are ready to go.

2. **Name Your Worksheets Correctly**

When it comes to Excel presentations it is mostly about clarity. The significance of a right and accurate project or worksheet name cannot be overstated for this single purpose. It may be an expression, a sentence, or just a single letter. Only make sure it is easy to grasp for you and everyone else with whom you will be sharing the file.

You must also be sure that the name of your file is different from the titles of other worksheets on your device. After all, what good will all the lessons you are going to practice today do, if you cannot locate the worksheet you used them on?

3. **Define Your Header/Title**

Anything can work with your header and title, but it must stand out. Your header should clearly communicate the viewer what the file is about at first glance.

To do this, use a bigger font, underline, and embolden your header. You can also use different colors. Make sure your title stands out while still matching with the template's color scheme and overall aesthetic appearance. For your header, you may also use a different readable.

4. Dos and Don'ts Of Fonts

Full transparency: Use a consistent font for your data; you may either use the same font for your header or modify it. To make your worksheet look professional, you should not use more than three fonts in a single presentation.

Font type

Readability should always be a priority. Sans-serif fonts are the right option for your Excel spreadsheet. Calibri, Arial, Helvetica, and Playfair are just a few of the many available fonts you can use. They will bring out the best of your Excel presentation, especially when used with the right spacing, alignment, and color.

DO: Calibri
DON'T: Curlz MT

Font size

Even though it usually depends on the presentation, font 12 with double spacing is often recommended to increase readability. As previously mentioned, the header font should be made larger. The headers should be bigger than the subleaders, which should be bigger than the data fonts.

Alignment

Excel's alignment feature is not used too much. If you want the presentation to appear professional, you will want to use the alignment feature to its full potential.

If the Alignment is easier at the side, headers should be aligned in the center. Numbers and numerical data should be aligned at the right, while texts must be aligned at the left. In the data input, center alignment is not recommended. To wrap your data or title around a cell, click it, then go to the Home toolbar, select Alignment, and then wrap your text.

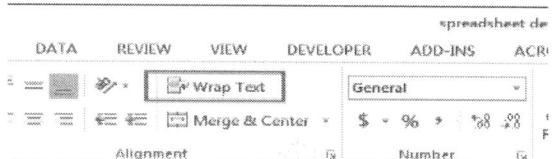

5. Create Space For Breathing Room

When you see a densely packed, clumsy and wordy text or spreadsheet, your brain gets bored reading it even before you begin. However, if the spreadsheet is separated into categories, it becomes more appealing to the eyes and easier for the brain to interpret.

The B2 rule is the solution: always begin your presentation on row 2 of column B, leaving the A column and the very first row blank.

Also, do not let the document's height and width autofit. Your workspace must enable you to be flexible and creative. Instead, manually change the height and width of the presentation so that it has only enough white space to readability.

6. Add An Image

Whether it's a picture, an abstract drawing, or a logo, images go a fair way toward improving your spreadsheet. Some of the stunning presentations you have seen, use images that make their presentations appear official and professional. A thousand words are expressed in pictures. Although Excel is not intended to provide the same presentation as PowerPoint, using an image can help you make the presentation more memorable.

7. Go Off the Grid

Do you acknowledge that erasing grid lines except those associated with your results would elicit questions about how you managed to do it and whether you use the same Excel program they do? Try it out today.

Go to the View tab that is located on the ribbon of your spreadsheet.

Uncheck the box in the Show section, next to gridlines.

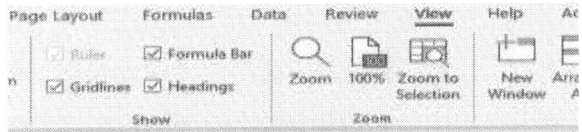

8. Zebra Striped

Rows are actually stacked on top of each other, zebra stripes are the alternating light and dark shades. This is beneficial in a variety of respects. For starters, it has a pleasing aesthetic that renders your work seem more organized, particularly if you are showing hundreds of rows of details. Second, it aids readability and correlation. A reader will follow a row from the far right to the far left without losing sight of which row he or she is looking at.

When you make a table in Excel, it will result zebra-striped by default (Tip: To create a table easily, pick the data and use shortcut ^ + T on a Mac or Ctrl + T on Windows). You can actually adjust the color and pattern of your zebra stripes on the Design page, under Table Styles.

If required, it can also be achieved with a formula in conditional formatting. Conditional formatting is achieved by emphasizing principles that meet those criteria (e.g., all odd-numbered rows). The painter method in the Home toolbar could be used to copy it from one cell to another.

9. Use Tables, Graphs, And Charts

Without any kind of visual representation, presentations are incomplete. You should visually reflect the raw data in the mediums that can be interpreted in a quick look, whether it is a graph, chart, or table. Graphs, charts, and tables are important tools to have, particularly if you have a lot of data that spans several columns and rows.

The graph, table, and chart features are just like symbiotic siblings in the Excel ecosystem.

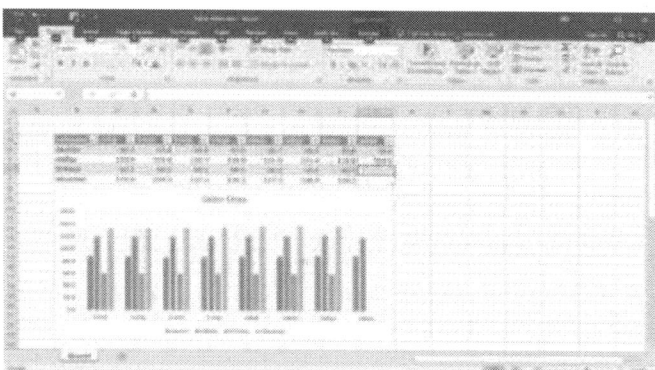

10. Create Cell Styles

Excel has actually a number of pre-defined cell styles. However, you may make your favorite custom styles. If you want to keep the visuals consistent, this option might be better than using a template. After you have created a stunning spreadsheet with the your data, save the style and use it in your future presentations too.

Simply pick the cells you want to save, then go to the Home toolbar, press "more" at the top of the style gallery, and then "new cell style." A style dialog box will appear, allowing you to name the style, change its properties, and save it.

Why alter something that is not broken and fits well? You can, though, introduce a little variety by switching up the color palette now and then.

11. Show Restraint

You have learned all of these pointers and are ready to begin your presentation; however, avoid overdoing it. To reach the "just enough" middle ground, you must navigate a delicate line between underwhelming and excessive. As in all, make sure the presentation is well balanced.

Bonus: Make Use of and Earn with Your Excel Skills in Workspace and Marketplace

What are the uses of Microsoft Excel in the workplace? Or in the marketplace? If we list of some of the ways that business uses MS Excel, its quite long. But we've broken it down to just a few.

MS Excel is used for a variety of tasks, including storing information, analyzing and sorting data, and reporting. Spreadsheets are incredibly popular in the corporate world because they are highly visual and relatively simple to use.

Business analysis, human resource management, performance reporting, and operations management are just a few of the many applications for Microsoft Excel that are often found in businesses. Because we analyzed employment data, we can say with certainty that (using MS Excel).

1. **Business Analysis**

Business analysis is the most popular usage of MS Excel at work.

Business analysis is fundamentally data-driven decision making. Businesses naturally collect data on product sales, website traffic, supply costs, insurance claims, etc.

Company analysis is the practice of making data relevant to business owners. You might, for example, run a profitability report by weekday. If the company consistently loses money on Sundays, management may use that data to make decisions (such as closing on Sundays).

2. **People Management**

One of the most actual common applications of Excel in company is to manage people.

Employees, clients, sponsors, or training participants may all be organized in MS Excel.

Personal data may be saved and accessed effectively with Excel. A spreadsheet row or column may include an individual's name, email address, employee start date, purchases, subscription status, and last contact.

3. **Office Administration**

Office administrators utilize Microsoft Excel to input and store critical administrative data. It is possible to utilize the same data for both accounting and financial reporting.

Excel is also essential in office administration for duties like invoicing, bill payment, and contacting suppliers and customers. It's a multi-purpose office management tool.

4. Project Management

An Excel Workbook can be a good alternative to PM software.

Projects are commercial activity with a budget and a timeline. Project plans may be entered into a workbook to monitor progress and keep the project on track.

Using Excel allows you to simply share the project workbook with others, particularly those unfamiliar with or unable to use proprietary PM software.

5. Managing Problems

Excel is an excellent program manager. It may be tailored to a particular program's needs. It's also easy to switch managers since MS Excel is commonly used.

Like a project, a program requires user input and may be ongoing. Manage resources, monitor progress and retain participant information using MS Excel.

6. Contract Administration

Contract administrators like to utilize Microsoft Excel since it is a simple and straightforward tool for documenting contract data, such as dates, milestones, deliverables, and payment amounts.

There are many different contract management templates available, and each of them may be customized to meet the specific contract type or stage of the contract lifecycle that is being used.

7. Account Management

Account managers must be proficient in MS Excel since they receive and maintain client records.

An account manager's role is to cultivate current customer connections. To increase client loyalty and repeat purchases. It's a marketing position and a popular MBA profession.

Excel is widely used in account administration because it allows easy file sharing and maintenance.

Learning Excel is a very tricky and complicated, I know. But it will be worth it for the number of new jobs you'll be able to apply to.

Not so sure if you want to pay money for Excel classes quite yet? You may change your mind when you see this list of careers that require it.

- Administrative Assistants
- Accountants
- Cost Estimator
- Project Manager
- Financial Analyst
- Business Analyst
- Data Analyst
- Information Clerk

These are some of the careers you might want to explore with using your Excel skills.

In fact, Excel is here to stay, and organizations will continue to rely on it as their main tool for a wide range of tasks and applications, ranging from information technology initiatives to workplace picnics.

A solid understanding of Excel is essential for the majority of office-based workers today, and improving one's Excel abilities may open the door to advancement and leadership chances in the workplace. Excel is a strong tool, but it cannot do all of the tasks on its own. It takes a competent computer user to take use of everything that Excel has to offer in order to provide the finest outcomes possible for their company's needs.

You just need to include your knowledge of Excel in your Resume! Make it interesting that you know it, and boom! You will be found as a person who will do their Excel work for them.

Conclusion

Microsoft Excel is a significant spreadsheet and data analyzing computer program with a broad range of capabilities. Different kinds of data can be organized, calculated and kept data saved for future use. Excel grid interface allows you to organize virtually any type of data you can think of. It is actually a powerful tool for performing analysis and what-if scenarios. To calculate the various circumstances, you employ formulas in a cell; make spreadsheets of your sales, charts for presenting your data.

In today's world, it has become an essential tool across the globe for many reasons. As excel is easy to use and an ability to add and remove information without causing any difficulty, MS Excel is frequently utilized for a wide range of tasks. When it comes to anything involving financial activity, Excel is a need. Making new spreadsheets with bespoke formulae for everything from a basic quarterly forecast to an entire corporate annual report makes Excel enticing for many people.

Excel is popular for organizing and monitoring common information like sales leads, project progress reports, contact lists, and billing. Finally, Excel comes in handy when working with huge datasets in science and statistics. Using Excel statistical formulae and graphing features, researchers may more easily do variance analysis and visualize large amounts of data. Microsoft Excel plays a vital role in so many industries. In the following departments, the importance of Microsoft Excel may be observed.

In this book, we have learned everything about Microsoft Excel, the Introduction of Microsoft excel, its history, its versions. We learned about its inference and Ribbon. The commands and buttons we can use to make our work easy from different tabs of the Ribbon. We learned to enter, edit, modify, sort, filter, and validate data. Concept of worksheet, cells, columns and rows. Everything about Excel formulas and functions in the easiest way possible is being explained in this book. Difference between functions and formulas and how to use them. Shortcuts for excel that can make you work fast and be done with it within minutes. Shortcuts are also being sorted according to your ease like there are shortcuts for editing, shortcuts for excel overall.

This book is your ultimate guide for Excel and will help you learn and work on Excel easily without any complications. This book is an accessible guide for day-to-day use and may help you learn this program in no time, whether you are a student, working, or retired.

Manufactured by Amazon.ca
Bolton, ON